LEGENDS
DON'T RETIRE

ISBN: 979-8-9868139-0-5

Cover & Illustrations by Ethan Chase Warner

Edited by Jennifer Liane Hunt

Olive Street Press
118 W Olive St
Keller, TX 76248
www.olivestreetpress.com

Disclosures

This book contains general information that may not be suitable for everyone. The information contained herein should not be construed as personalized investment advice. Past performance is no guarantee of future results. There is no guarantee that the views and opinions expressed in this newsletter will come to pass. Investing in the stock market involves gains and losses and may not be suitable for all investors. Information presented herein is subject to change without notice and should not be considered as a solicitation to buy or sell any security.

Neither Triad Hybrid Advisors nor Bluegrass Legacy Group offer legal or tax advice. Please consult the appropriate professional regarding your individual circumstance.

Securities offered through Triad Advisors, LLC., Member FINRA/SIPC. Advisory Services offered through Triad Hybrid Solutions, LLC., a registered investment advisor. Bluegrass Legacy Group and Triad Advisors, LLC are not affiliated.

Not associated with or endorsed by the Social Security Administration or any other government agency.

Hypothetical examples are for illustrative purposes only and are not intended to represent the past or future performance of any specific investment. Actual results will fluctuate with market conditions and will vary over time.

Table of Contents

From the entire team at Bluegrass Legacy Group, thank you for purchasing this book. We are committed to help families, businesses, and non-profits steward their resources and define a lasting legacy that influences the communities where they live and work.

As a sign of our gratitude, we would like to offer you a complimentary **Work Optional Lifestyle Starter Kit**. Complete with checklists, templates, videos, and guides, this resource is designed to empower a path toward financial confidence and making the impact you desire.

To request your kit, contact us at kyle@legendsdontretire.com and let us know you are ready to define your legacy!

Acknowledgements

To my clients, thank you for trusting me and the Bluegrass Legacy team with stewarding your respective legacies. It is an honor to serve you every day. Your confidence in us even during difficult times is truly humbling.

To my team, I appreciate your diligence and support in building Bluegrass. Your daily commitment to our clients and our values is remarkable. This is by far the best place I have ever had the pleasure of working, and it truly would not be a reality without you. I give you my sincere gratitude.

To Mike Scoma, thank you for introducing me to this industry, neighbor. It has opened an entire world I didn't even realize existed. You saw something in me before anyone else, and you have changed the trajectory of my life and my family's life.

To Jennifer Hunt, thank you for joining me on yet another literary adventure. Your virtual red pen hurts, but it's exactly what is needed to redeem my words. You are my editorial armor-bearer.

To my review squad—Timothy Paulson, Bryan Flanagan, Tommy Earp, Kevin Schneider, Shane Bender, Suzanne Castle, Kati Gabhart, and Justin Winstead—thank you for your early feedback, which was instrumental in shaping this book's content and message.

To my six children, thank you for giving me a purpose bigger than myself. You all are the "legacy" in Bluegrass Legacy Group, and I am so grateful for each of you.

To Parker, thank you for making me a "BG" (Bluegrass/Bald Guy/Bodacious Grandpa/Big Goof). I know in time there will be more grandkiddos, but you'll always be the first. I love you, little man.

To my mother, thank you for giving me unconditional love. It is the greatest gift you could ever give me. I would not be where I am today without you.

To my father, I miss you dearly. I am truly grateful for the thirty-nine years we had together and all the things you invested in me. Your soul is woven into every fiber of Bluegrass Legacy Group and this book.

To Tammy, you are the love of my life. Thank you for being so patient as we built Bluegrass Legacy Group together. It hasn't been an easy journey, but having you by my side has made it so much more bearable. You are the best thing that's ever happened to me. I love you.

Foreword

Imagine sitting around a crackling campfire on a cool and calm night under billions of glistening stars, sipping your favorite drink as the sounds of nature hum in the background. You're there in that circle with those you care about deeply and enjoy immensely, evident by the laughs belted out in between stories.

As the others turn in for their rest, you remain—staring into the fire, poking it occasionally, pondering all the goodness in your life and thinking about how blessed you are to have lived the life you've lived.

In between the daily chores of maintaining a home, growing a family, and ongoing obligations at work—all while striving for healthy friendships and a healthy body—you have managed to fill the decades with adventures and challenges in a multitude of places and with a wide array of unique characters. You're not done yet, but you are nearing the final chapters of this epic journey, and what a journey it has been.

As you reflect on this, there is a peace that surpasses understanding. It hasn't been all perfect, and you made mistakes, yet you feel confident that you are a winner. You have fought the good fight and ran the race with endurance, and you have come through victorious. The sacrifices and disciplines you made to create the life you once so desperately hoped and prayed for have paid off. Your investments financially and relationally compounded, and the return is sweet. The longing that once burned deep inside and seemed like a distant dream is now a reality.

Well done. . .

This vision of sitting around the fire and proudly looking back on our lives is one of the many things Kyle and I share. When we met years ago, each respectively building our early businesses, we felt a kinship and a connection of shared values that bonded us almost immediately. We were both committed to playing the game of life and would not be content sitting on the sidelines or in the stands, and we didn't want to just play the game—but to win it.

Both of us burn with a desire to live a significant life that *really* matters and continues to matter, even when we're gone. We strongly believe that each person has a purpose and mission that goes beyond merely existing; we aren't striving to survive but thrive. Among our greatest hopes is to leave a legacy of meaningful influence.

Over time as Kyle and I have grown personally and professionally, he has consistently inspired me with creative ideas and practical solutions. He has encouraged me to create habits, goals, and disciplines that have not only helped me accomplish more but become more of who I am meant to be. In addition to being an investor and entrepreneur, I am also a life and business coach. Much of what I'm doing as a coach is paying forward the type of help I have received from countless individuals, of whom Kyle is among the best.

And that is what this book is largely about. It's about those seemingly mundane things we often do, like making a good purchase or setting money aside for retirement. It's about the seeds we are planting now that seem small, yet contain greater potential than we can conceive. It's about impacting people who in turn impact more people.

Throughout this book, Kyle will encourage and inspire you like he has so many others. Although there are lots of words about numbers and dollars and money, all of which are necessary and important, it's ultimately not about that. This book is about who you are and who you want to become. It's about creating a life you love and building a legacy that lifts others up even after you have passed on.

Leaving a meaningful legacy does not accidentally happen to people who happen to be in the right spot at the right time. Of course, people who become legends are met with opportunity — but to take advantage of that opportunity, one must possess the right plan, practices, principles, and passion to bring it to successful completion. In *Legends Don't Retire*, Kyle offers us all of these and more, and he guides us to creating a more enjoyable and meaningful life for ourselves and others.

In contrast to the opening story, imagine yourself sitting by a fire looking back with regret over the missed opportunities and unrealized potential, bemoaning the times you chose the superficial and temporary over the significant and eternal, wishing you could do it all over again. You realize that in a quest for contentment, you became complacent. You didn't leave it all on the field. You didn't do what you should have done. Your voice and your life faded quietly.

Oh, what could have been! Friend, don't let this be you.

Read this book, receive its encouragement, and apply its principles, and you will leave a legendary legacy!

Sincerely,

Justin Winstead
Life & Business Coach
Entrepreneur
https://improver.coach

Who Should Read This Book

This book is for you if:

- You want to live and leave a legacy that is bigger than yourself.
- The traditional view of retirement seems outdated or unappealing to you.
- You are concerned about running out of money during your lifetime.
- There is a purpose and a passion inside of you that needs a roadmap to follow.

This book is not for you if:

- You have already retired and you are loving it.
- You want to work tirelessly the rest of your life.
- You plan to trust Social Security as your sole source of income when you retire from working.
- Knitting and playing bridge for the rest of your life is your idea of time well spent.

If this describes you, please kindly pass this book along to someone who could benefit from a fresh perspective on work, retirement, and legacy building.

My Commitment to You

I want to make a few commitments to you:

- **Straight talk.** In the pages of this book, you'll receive straight talk about goal setting, financial planning, and the inherent risks within the classic approach to retirement in the US.
- **Varied content.** I will share truth, a little math, and plenty of examples and analogies to make the content approachable.
- **Tough love.** I will shed light and challenge your assumptions about money, work/life balance, and financial planning.
- **Provide insight.** I will share insight that most financial planners and advisors do not mention.
- **Share knowledge.** I will offer my best effort to educate and empower you to map your ideal life and legacy.

I also want you to know what you won't get with this book:

- **No sales pitch.** My goal is to educate and empower. You can implement my strategies yourself or with your current advisor.
- **No jargon.** As much as possible, I'm going to avoid industry terminology and confusing economic verbiage.
- **No math lessons.** While there will be a few financial illustrations and investing principles given, this book isn't about formulas and equations. It's meant to be practical and actionable.

Bluegrass Values

Bluegrass Legacy Group centers around seven core values that underlie our perspective and advice. These are referenced throughout the book.

1. **People first. Money second.** (*Relationship*)

   Our first commitment is to see our clients, partners, and other team members as people. If we take care of the people, the money will follow.

2. **One thing = everything.** (*Excellence*)

   Everything we do reflects our attention to detail and concern for quality. Strive for excellence in everything.

3. **Honor to serve.** (*Gratitude*)

   Clients entrust us with their life savings, their hopes and dreams, and their most intimate life details. Our calling is a noble one, and we should embrace each day and each relationship with grateful hearts.

4. **Manage expectations, not money.** (*Counsel*)

   While money management is our responsibility, it is secondary. The most important thing we manage is our clients' and partners' expectations to achieve realistic, sustainable outcomes.

5. **Small promises.** *(Integrity)*

   Trust is earned. We make small promises every day. In time, clients and partners will give us the opportunity to make larger promises on their behalf.

6. **Full glasses. Bigger pies.** *(Vision)*

   In a world full of pessimism and fears of scarcity, we embrace each challenge with optimism and a mindset of abundance. We focus on solutions rather than problems and collaborate with others in our industry rather than competing with them.

7. **Call your mother.** *(Appreciation)*

   Show appreciation toward everyone who has been instrumental in getting you where you are today. Never outgrow a client or partner. Call your mother.

Introduction

When I was a kid, my mother would take me shopping with her. We might have been gone only a few hours, but it felt like an eternity. While on those trips, I developed a hobby. As we would pass payphones* and vending machines, I checked every coin return. When time allowed, I would drop to the ground and look for stray coins. Eventually I carried a ruler with me to scrape the floor under the machines and retrieve every coin. My mother was horrified by how dirty I got, but my efforts were effective. One day I gathered ten dollars in loose change. It wasn't much on an hourly basis, but at the ripe old age of eight, I felt accomplished.

In addition to my change-gathering enterprise, I frequently did jobs around the house and brainstormed ways to generate money. I asked everyone I met what they did for a living and routinely researched different career paths and their earning potential. Considering I was taught to store up treasures in heaven and not on Earth,† I feared this fascination with wealth, but in time I discovered it was not driven by greed or envy but

---

*Many moons ago, we didn't carry tiny computers in our pockets. If you wanted to talk with someone, you used a phone attached to the wall. When in public, there were booths where you inserted coins (physical money made from metal) to make a call. Hopefully the person you called was within earshot of another wall phone. Otherwise, you would be out of luck. Those were dark times.

†Matthew 6:19–21

by a desire to produce value and unlock potential. As a financial planner, I've seen how wealth allows us to impact our families and communities. But as Spider-Man's Uncle Ben stated in the iconic 2002 film, "With great power comes great responsibility."[1] Consequently, I see it as my mission to help families, businesses, and nonprofits steward their resources well and turn lives into legacies.

Throughout the book, I'm going to address problems I've encountered with the classic perspective on retirement. Too often, retirees forego their potential and settle for less because that's what everyone else has done. I'll also help you chart a path toward a Work Optional Lifestyle, which I have found more realistic and fulfilling than simply working for decades and hoping your nest egg will last.

Here's a quick glimpse into what is in store:

- The retirement landscape has changed, so you need a **fresh perspective** (*Chapter 1: There is No Gold Watch*).
- You need a **purpose,** not just a pastime (*Chapter 2: All Play and No Work Makes Jack a Dull Boy*).
- You need a **roadmap,** not an arbitrary number (*Chapter 3: There is No Magic Number*).
- We are wired for **growth** but sometimes stop short of our greatest potential (*Chapter 4: Evolve, Don't Retire*).
- You have a **story to live** (*Chapter 5: Legacy Should Be Lived, Not Just Left*).

- Your life is **dynamic,** and your planning should be too (*Chapter 6: The Anti-Retirement Plan*).
- You can never do by learning, but you can always **learn by doing** (*Chapter 7: A Plan in Motion*).

Thank you for taking the time to walk down this path with me for a bit. I wish you all the best on your journey.

With gratitude,

Chapter One
There Is No Gold Watch

The trouble with being in the rat race is that even if you win,

you're still a rat.

—Lily Tomlin

On September 6, 1874, Ida May Fuller was born into a Vermont farming family with a lineage traced back to the original passengers on *The Mayflower*. Ida served as a schoolteacher, a legal secretary, and an active member in the local Baptist church in Ludlow, Vermont. She lived to be 100 years old. Her life was notable for a variety of reasons, but she is most famous for a check that was issued to her on January 31, 1940, in the amount of $22.54. It was the first monthly retirement benefit issued by the newly formed Social Security Administration.

By every possible analysis, Ms. Fuller received a phenomenal return from her rather meager investment into this newly formed federal system. She worked for only three years under the Social Security program and paid a whopping $24.75 in taxes on her earnings. Yet throughout her lifetime, she managed to cash checks totaling $22,888.92.[1] Sign me up!

Things have changed since Ida collected her first monthly check. Average life expectancy in the U.S. has increased from 62.07 years in 1940 to 78.81 years in 2020. The number of workers paying into Social Security in 1940 outnumbered beneficiaries by 159.[2] In the modern era, there are fewer than three workers contributing for every person receiving benefits.[3] Since 1940, inflation has eroded the value of the US dollar by 3.70% annually, for a cumulative inflation of 1,799.05%.[4] So we're living longer, with fewer workers paying into a system designed during a different era with drastically different assumptions.

Looking beyond the Social Security system, the employment landscape has changed as well. Previous generations could count on finding a reliable employer, working for thirty-plus years, and retiring with a pension and a gold watch. In the modern era, it is rare to find an employer still offering a pension plan, and employees commonly work under multiple employers either because of layoffs or career progression. Consequently, funding your golden years rests squarely on your own shoulders.

HA!

Legends Learn to Laugh

I'm very proud of my gold pocket watch. My grandfather, on his deathbed, sold me this watch. —Woody Allen

Early in my journey, I worked with a variety of financial services organizations, including banks, pension funds (state and municipal), rating agencies, and insurance companies. I learned that while access to robust, employer-sponsored plans was commonplace twenty years ago, times have changed. With the growing financial burden of maintaining sponsored pension plans, employers have been forced to take drastic measures to maintain solvency. They have reduced benefits, increased qualification requirements, or even eliminated plans altogether.

Alongside the unreliability of traditional retirement assets, we are also living longer, thanks to advances in medicine and technology. DNA testing can prescribe nutrition uniquely tailored to someone's genome. Wearable devices monitor our sleep cycles and the number of steps we take every day. Medical conditions that were once fatal are increasingly manageable. We have more knowledge and more information at our fingertips than previous generations. Even our overall health awareness has improved dramatically.

Hydrate Don't Die-drate

As I'm typing this book, I have a 32-ounce reusable water bottle beside me, inscribed with motivational messages designed to encourage water consumption. It progresses from "get started" to "remember your goal," "keep chugging," and "don't give up." Furthermore, I have set a goal to drink two to four full bottles every day. If I were writing this book in the 80s, I'd more likely have a Coke next to me. I now know cigarettes are bad, hydration is crucial, sugar contributes to cancer, and sun exposure should be moderated. I'm still not sure whether I should eat eggs (the answer seems to change every few years).

With the heightened awareness around nutrition and the sophistication of modern medicine, we are living longer and healthier lives. While centenarians (individuals who live to be 100 years or older) make up a small percentage of the overall population, according to Pew Research, that proportion is growing. In 1990 there were 2.9 centenarians for every 10,000 adults ages sixty-five and older around the world. That share grew to 7.4 by 2015 and is projected to rise to 23.6 by 2050, amounting to an *eight-fold increase* in the span of only sixty years.[5] That's an impressive feat and allows an incredible opportunity to enjoy life and both reap from our elders and bestow wisdom to our own descendants, but it also adds even more pressure to the golden years of one's life.

Centenarians Per 10,000 Adults

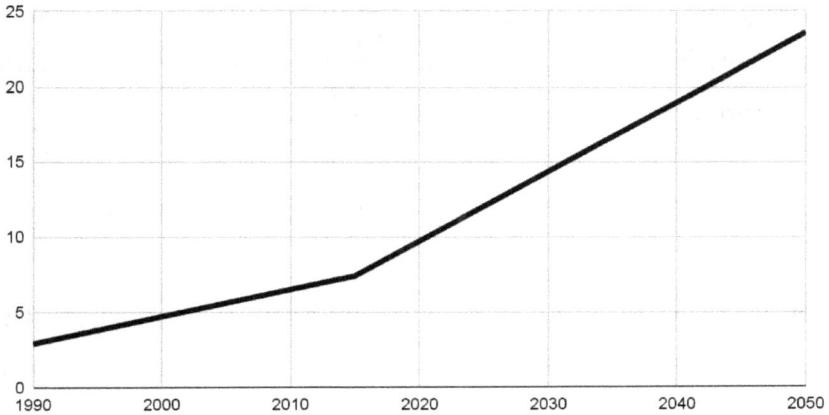

FIGURE 1. THE PERCENTAGE OF OUR POPULATION WHO WILL REACH OR EXCEED 100 YEARS OLD IS INCREASING DRAMATICALLY.

We're living substantially longer and healthier lives, and we're doing so with an increasingly less reliable financial framework.

It's a Marathon, Not a Sprint

As a financial planner and wealth advisor, I've had the opportunity to work with individuals, families, and small businesses navigating the complexities of retirement planning in the modern era. While previous generations could rely upon a combination of Social Security and employer-sponsored pension plans to meet their limited retirement needs for a few years, the picture today is more complicated. Because we're living longer, healthier lives, we expect to thrive longer than a handful of years after leaving traditional employment. Today's retiree must navigate a retirement roadmap spanning twenty-plus years without the resources sufficient for the journey. There's no gold watch. You aren't going to get some grand send-off from your employer. You're going to have to do more with less and for much longer than perhaps you originally imagined.

Avoiding the Retirement Trap

Even if you could manage to save enough to support your post-employment years, I don't believe we're wired to retire and fill our remaining days golfing, fishing, knitting, and playing bridge. While these hobbies can be enjoyable, if we aren't challenged and engaged, we tend to grow tired of the monotony and lack of stimulation.

Retirement is often considered some sort of inalienable right, but it is actually a contrived concept. In 1883 Otto von Bismarck believed industrialization would solidify Germany's place in the world. This would require constructing factories, employing a vast sum of workers, and ensuring the stability of the labor pool. He observed that unemployed young men were most likely to become social revolutionaries, so he proposed a system of social reform and provision for the elderly. This would ensure the exit of older workers and provide opportunities for the next generation of laborers to step in, keeping them too preoccupied to be distracted by political dissention or revolt. Thus he announced forced retirement, including a government pension, for anyone over age sixty-five.[6]

Dan Sullivan has served as a personal development coach and mentor for more than four decades. He is the founder and CEO of The Strategic Coach, Inc., a global movement of entrepreneurs and visionaries. He describes what he calls the *retirement trap,* which so many unwittingly fall into. "One of the most important things you can do for yourself is avoid the whole notion of retirement," he notes. "The entire idea of retirement means that you're no longer growing, no longer useful, and simply getting ready to die. Why would you think this way at all?"[7]

Just think for a moment about the word *retirement.* What springs to mind? What else do we *retire?*

Race horses.

Battleships.

Factory equipment.

We retire things when they are used up. We put them out to pasture when they are no longer useful. How appealing does that sound when applied to your life? Are you done being useful? I highly doubt it.

Out to Pasture?

We retire things when they are used up and no longer useful. Your career might end, but aren't you more than your job?

Humanity desires purpose and meaning. Each of us wants to make a difference, but we often allow a fearful, scarcity mindset to keep us from our full potential.

Legendary Questions

1. What assumptions have you made about the concept of retirement that may need to be reevaluated?

2. At what age would you consider yourself to be old and needing to slowing down?

3. When you think about the future, are you afraid of what might happen or excited about the possibilities?

Chapter Two
All Play and No Work Makes Jack a Dull Boy

The key is not to prioritize what's on your schedule,
but to schedule your priorities.
—Stephen Covey

I n the 1980 cult classic, *The Shining*, Jack Torrance mentally unravels as cabin fever sets in and he loses touch with reality. At one point, Jack's wife, Wendy, finds his manuscript with the phrase "all work and no play makes Jack a dull boy," written over and over. While excessive work can be damaging to one's psyche, the reverse is equally true. "All play" and "no work" is also unhealthy.

We are wired for work. In our innermost being we desire to be a productive member of our community, to pull our own weight and contribute. Nobody wants to be a drain on others. Being productive personally and professionally provides tremendous satisfaction. Whether you find your spark through a commercial vocation or a passionate avocation, purpose and productivity are essential to emotional well-being.

I love to travel. My wife and I build our calendar around restful vacations that allow us to escape the daily grind and recharge our batteries. But I can't stay on the charger indefinitely. After a couple weeks or sometimes even a few days, I need to return to normal life and contribute to my family, ministries, and my team.

HA!

Legends Learn to Laugh

The problem with retirement is you never get a day off. —Anonymous Dad

Over the years, I've coached hundreds of people pursuing their retirement goals. Many aspire to have more free time to travel, play golf, and relax. This is wonderful in theory, but walking away from work isn't as easy as it seems. Time and time again, I've seen people who retire with this idea only to find themselves restless and searching for a new direction six months later. The absence of purpose and daily motivation presents an unfamiliar challenge for many retirees. Few are prepared to effectively navigate this new chapter in their lives. I've told clients countless times—retiring is easy, but *staying retired* is the tricky part.

Lessons COVID Taught Us

In the spring of 2020, the entire world was forced into a simulated retirement. As COVID spread like wildfire, the world locked down and we quarantined in our homes. Our social and work calendars were suddenly vacant. It was fun at first. Pajama pants and Zoom meetings became the norm. At-home movie nights and board games became everyday activities. Stores quickly sold out of bicycles as people took advantage of their abundant free time. We were certainly afforded some incredible opportunities to reflect on our priorities and reconnect with our families. But eventually, we grew restless. Many simply could not cope with the vacuum created by a forced quarantine. After a few weeks of taking "retirement" for a spin, the novelty wore off, and we were eager to return to the normal life of schedules and obligations. We are wired for productivity and for purpose, and their absence leaves us feeling lost. COVID taught us a lot about ourselves, our society, and how much we depend upon work and community for our well-being. It also forced many of us to reevaluate our life choices. Consider the lessons we learned from this monumental event:

1. We aren't very good at doing nothing.
2. Work shouldn't be a crutch for our identity, but many of us don't know who we are without it.
3. Our social fabric is more fragile than we'd like to admit.

4. Pajama pants can serve as legitimate work attire in a Zoom-enabled business world.

5. Relationships are our most valuable resource, but our investment in them doesn't always reflect this.

6. Life is too short to pour two thousand-plus hours a year into a job that doesn't energize you.

7. When we are faced with a global health crisis, our priorities become clear, enabling us to reevaluate our daily investment of time and energy (hence "The Great Resignation").

People First, Money Second

COVID forced us to slow down and take a hard look in the mirror. We shuffled our priorities and reevaluated our goals, and although we have returned to a new version of normal, we carry the lessons we learned and the perspective we gained. COVID gave us a unique glimpse into the slowdown that occurs during retirement. Reflecting on these lessons, I aim to build my business with an emphasis on people, purpose, and passion.

The Bluegrass Legacy Group team strives to foster a people-first culture where team members are whole, energized, motivated, and valued. The first of our seven core values at Bluegrass is *People First, Money Second*, originally stated to underscore the importance of taking care of our clients regardless of their net worth or the size of their partnership with us. Over time, however, I realized the significance of applying this principle to caring for our Bluegrass team members. Billionaire Richard Bronson famously characterized it this way: "Clients do not come first. Employees come first. If you take care of your employees, they will take care of the clients."

We live out this commitment in big and small ways. One example is our policy for time away from work. Rather than tracking or accruing time off, we enforce mandatory and unlimited paid time off for all team members themselves, requiring a minimum of two days off per quarter (but encouraging more time away).

One of the most popular benefits is a one-month paid sabbatical every four years. This encourages our team to develop a cadence of stepping away from the business several times throughout their career to gain perspective on their priorities and insight into who they are. During this crucial practice, we enforce the following sabbatical rules:

- **No Contact.** Employees must completely remove themselves from work for the entire month, including the office, phone, Slack, email, LinkedIn, etc.
- **One Month.** The entire month must be consecutive (i.e., you can't take four mini-vacations in lieu of the sabbatical).
- **With Purpose.** While the obvious delegation of professional responsibilities must be done in advance of the sabbatical, we also encourage personal preparation to ensure purpose and intentionality, not just idle time away.

Each sabbatical element creates a unique, compelling experience that transforms the individual, the team, and even the business as a whole.

The first rule, *No Contact*, allows the individual to completely disconnect for an extended time. No communication or connection with the team is permitted. We are drowning in notifications, alerts, reminders, and a never-ending pile of tasks, and the temptation to get sucked back into the whirlwind is simply too strong to resist. Complete separation for a full month is the only option. That's why I recommend starting the sabbatical by traveling somewhere else (ideally someplace with terrible Wi-Fi) and maintaining physical distance.

Secondly, the *One Month* rule strengthens the team by necessitating cross-training. If someone is only gone for a week, the team can easily kick the proverbial can down the road. Client requests can be deferred until the team member returns. Realistic expectations can be set about when a task will be completed or a response provided. It's easy to dismiss the small gap in time. You can't do that for an entire month. When it's a full month, the team must find a way to creatively fill the void and maintain business operations. Doing so encourages a critical look at processes and workflow. Are there opportunities for more efficiency? Can we improve systems to reduce individual backlogs? Is every step crucial, or have we been doing certain things because we've always done it that way?

While the team and the business grow stronger, the benefits to the person on sabbatical are even greater. For the first week or two, you can contentedly rest and relax. But by the third week, you are faced with yourself and what to do with this time and freedom. Who are you in the absence of your job? What defines your identity beyond your professional image? Most people don't confront these kinds of questions routinely. The sabbatical forces you to reflect and define yourself differently than society defines you.

Thirdly, the entire experience should be *On Purpose*, necessitating the creation of a plan rather than just winging it. Advance planning prepares the business for this team member's absence. Defining Standard Operating Procedures (SOPs), developing contingency plans, cross-training other team members, and learning to effectively document are natural by-products of this approach. All of this lays the groundwork for evaluating the business and ensuring each person is used for their highest and best purpose. But the purposeful planning isn't just for the business. It also directs the individual to approach the sabbatical with intent. You create a plan for learning, growing, exploring, and recharging. This doesn't mean you follow a strict schedule every day, but it does establish some structure, a few goals, and mental preparation for an extended period of reflection and self-discovery.

You may not have the luxury of a sabbatical, but the lessons are important for anyone looking to refresh and recharge. The principle of *No Contact* underscores the importance of a true break from your professional life. The principle of *One Month* highlights the importance of significant, sustained distance from your work. That could be several days off work between a couple of weekends and a federal holiday. However you achieve your days off, the most important principle is *On Purpose*. Anyone can lay on the beach and do nothing. Intentionally infusing your time away from work requires preparation and planning to create a conducive environment for growth and self-exploration. This valuable exercise offers you a brief glimpse into the importance of having a plan and a purpose during retirement.

Living a Legacy

I often discuss the notion of legacy with friends, family, and clients. It's in my firm's name and it's in my blood. From these conversations, I have noticed two prevailing interpretations of the word.

Many believe legacy is something you bequeath. Merriam-Webster's defines *legacy* as a gift of property or anything handed down from the past.[1] These definitions refer to an inheritance and leaving something behind after you're gone.

Others think a legacy only applies to those who amass a significant pool of assets. This mindset attaches legacy to statues, hospital wings, and libraries, presuming a lasting legacy requires an elite level of philanthropy reserved for only extremely affluent families.

Both concepts, while valid, miss the true potential buried within each of us. Legacy calls us to engage in a lifetime of discovery. It beckons us to learn who we are and what we have to offer our loved ones and the causes we want to magnify. While influence can be made through wealth, it extends beyond money alone. Your legacy is a story of significance that you write upon the hearts of people you care about and weave into the fabric of organizations you support.

Elements of Your Legacy

- Assets you pass on
- Businesses you build
- Causes you champion
- Ministries you promote
- Organizations you support
- People you touch
- Projects you launch
- Values and priorities you embody
- Wisdom and insight you share

Defining LEGACY

Your legacy is the sum of the life you live and the impact you make on your community and the people around you.

Each person's idea of legacy may differ, but everyone's legacy develops from a lifetime of choices they make, people and organizations they invest in, and the wisdom they transfer to the next generation.

While wealth can certainly magnify your influence, it is not the essence of your legacy but more of an amplifier. Your legacy is the sum of the life you have lived and the impact you make on your community and the people around you. Many talk about leaving a legacy. I prefer to focus on *living* one.

Work Optional Lifestyle

By now you've likely come to realize I'm not a huge fan of traditional retirement scenarios. It's problematic mathematically as well as psychologically. Furthermore, it has the nasty side effect of delaying the most important aspect of life: living a legacy. The classic notion of retirement promotes a deeply flawed model in which you work tirelessly for decades in order to enjoy your golden years. Unfortunately, this can result in missed opportunities to enjoy life, invest in relationships, and build a legacy. There's a tendency to associate legacy with the end of your life, but as consultant and coach Peter Strople puts it, "Legacy is not leaving something for people. It's leaving something in people."[2]

The model we coach many of our clients to embrace at Bluegrass Legacy Group is what we call a Work Optional Lifestyle. It's about structuring your assets, income streams, and spending needs in such a way that you are no longer dependent upon a traditional full-time job to maintain your lifestyle. Instead, you can pursue work you enjoy, invest time and energy in your passions, and experience true freedom of choice. Best of all, this doesn't hinge on the same sort of arbitrary timeline that traditional retirement strategies embrace (e.g., retirement at age 59.5, 62, 67, etc.).

Defining WORK OPTIONAL LIFESTYLE

Balancing your expenses with sources of income such that paid employment is a choice rather than a necessity.

With a Work Optional Lifestyle, you simply maintain relatively modest spending goals in accordance with your income (some sources could be passive while others may still involve work, but it's by choice). This same counterculture mindset is the heartbeat behind the Financial Independence, Retire Early (FIRE) movement inspired by the 1992 best-selling book *Your Money or Your Life*,[3] which argues for radical frugality, aggressive savings, and careful planning. By saving 50–70% of your income, amassing twenty-five to thirty times your annual expenses, and creating a modest plan for drawing on your assets annually, FIRE advocates independence. This relatively small, grassroots movement has gained traction more recently. Coming out of the Great Recession (2008) and now the Great Resignation (2020), the FIRE community has built momentum and a cult following. Author Kristy Shen notes, "FIRE allows people to choose how they want to spend their time rather than be forced to spend their time at work."[4]

Whoa! Saving seventy percent of your annual income? Radical frugality? That's a bit extreme. I agree. It's not for everyone. FIRE's primary limitation is the reliance upon stockpiling cash and passive index investments. I recommend a more balanced strategy in which your income streams include real estate, rising dividends, business interests, and supplemental consulting income.

Multiple Streams of Income

Income can be generated through real estate, rising dividends, business interests, consulting, and side hustles.

Most financial advisors love to talk about the importance of diversification in building a portfolio. While this is important, it's only part of the story. It's equally important to apply diversification to other aspects of your strategy, such as tax diversification and income diversification.

What if you prefer a classic retirement and you're capable of saving enough to last through an extended retirement? That's fantastic. More power to you. Just remember that math is only half the equation. The other half is your emotional well-being. Are you prepared for the freedom of retirement? Is your identity tied up with your work? I often advise clients, "It's important that you don't just retire *from* something. It's important you retire *to* something."

We're wired for productivity. It doesn't matter if you pour yourself into a ministry, your community, or a passion project, but you need something other than golfing, fishing, and traveling to keep yourself stimulated. If you don't want to meet the same fate as Jack Torrance in *The Shining*, it's important to approach your post-career life with a plan and a purpose.

Legendary Questions

1. When was the last time you significantly separated yourself from work and busyness? What did you learn about yourself?

2. If you had an entire month with no obligations, what would you do with your time and energy?

3. What aspects of your legacy do you envision cultivating throughout your life

Chapter Three
There is No Magic Number

Torture numbers, and they'll confess to anything.

—*Gregg Easterbrook*

During my formative years in the 1980s, financial goals were pretty simple. Find a way to earn six figures ($100K+) and you'd be set. If you could accumulate a million dollars, you'll never want for anything. If only it were that simple. Thanks to the ravages of inflation, those figures no longer bear themselves out. Perhaps more importantly, your desired lifestyle (e.g., spending, travel, entertainment) has a dramatic effect on the viability of any savings target. There is no magic number. Everyone's situation is unique. Despite this, people frequently ask me for an arbitrary number.

"Hey Kyle, my golfing buddy told me I need to save three million in order to be comfortable. Does that sound about right?"

"You know, Kyle, my husband and I don't go on fancy trips or do much shopping, so I can't imagine us needing more than a few hundred thousand for retirement. I mean, that's a lot of money."

I get it. It's hard to wrap our brains around what we will need for decades of unemployment (which traditional retirement equates to). Time and inflation, as well as unpredictable variables, will affect everyone, and there's no way to provide an arbitrary, off-the-cuff answer that works for each person's situation. Allow me to reiterate: *there is no magic number*. Everyone's situation is unique.

Compound Interest Can Be Magical

However, numbers can still be magical, especially when you compound those numbers over time. There's a terrific quote that has been attributed to Albert Einstein: "Compound interest is the eighth wonder of the world. He who understands it, earns it; he who doesn't, pays it." While there are some who question whether Einstein originated this quote or even if he ever said it, the power of compound interest is evident.[1]

A phenomenally powerful mechanism, compound interest gains momentum over time. "Compounding happens when earnings on your savings are reinvested to generate their own earnings," says Kate Ryan, a director of investment solutions at TIAA. "Those, in turn, are reinvested to generate their own earnings and so on. So over time, compounding can add a lot of value because you have more time periods—more earnings—and those earnings are 'earning earnings.'"[2]

Defining COMPOUND INTEREST

Compounding is when your money gets a job and works *for* you to make more. As this cycle repeats, growth accelerates.

Compound Interest Scenario #1: Tax-Free Bucket

Macey invests $500 per month into a Roth IRA every year for twenty-five years. The account compounds throughout the year, averaging 7%* over time. After twenty-five years, the account grows to $407,530.64. She continues to invest for ten more years, and the value more than doubles to $907,486.03. That's the power of compounding.[3]

Because Macey invested through a Roth IRA, the dollars she contributed were part of her normal after-tax income. Since every dollar contributed had already been taxed, she will access the proceeds tax-free in retirement (assuming she follows Roth rules). Throughout twenty-five years, she paid tax on the original $150K she invested, but she has over $250K tax-free. Assuming she continues for another decade, it gets even better. In thirty-five

---

*Averages are a funny beast. You could be up double digits two years in a row, nearly flat the third year, up again the fourth, and negative the fifth. But for planning purposes, we talk in terms of an average return over time.

years, she paid tax on $210K and has nearly $700K that avoids tax entirely.

Compound Interest Scenario #2: The Earlier The Better

Even if you only invest for ten years of your working life, *when* you start makes an enormous difference. Consider three siblings: Alex, Kati, and Drew,* who each invest consistently every month for a decade. The dramatic variation in their totals are a result of the differences in the duration of their investing.

- Alex invests $500 a month from age twenty-five to thirty-five and then stops. He has contributed $60K, compounded at 7% annually, so he will have $88,056 at age thirty-five. If he does not withdraw, does not make another contribution, and allows the compounding to continue, he'll have $540,254 by age sixty.
- At age thirty-five, Kati starts investing $500 a month and continues for the next twenty-five years. She contributes a total of $150K, compounded at 7% annually, so she will have $410,312 by age sixty.

---

*This scenario is special for a couple reasons. Kati, Alex, and Drew are three of my children, as is Macey from Scenario #1 as well as Avery and Garon who appear later. To re-create scenario #2, use the online calculator referenced in the Notes at the end of the book. Kati and Drew's illustrations can be re-created easily. Alex's illustration will require two steps. First, determine the initial investment period. Then use the compounded total as the initial deposit in the second scenario where you don't contribute anything at all. You can use the same calculator in the Notes section to make these calculations.

- Drew doesn't get started until he turns fifty. He knows he has a lot of time to make up for, so he invests $1000 a month. In ten years, he has contributed $120K, compounded at 7% annually, so he will have $176,112 by age sixty.

Alex started early and only invested for ten years. His siblings started later, invested more, and they are never able to catch up.

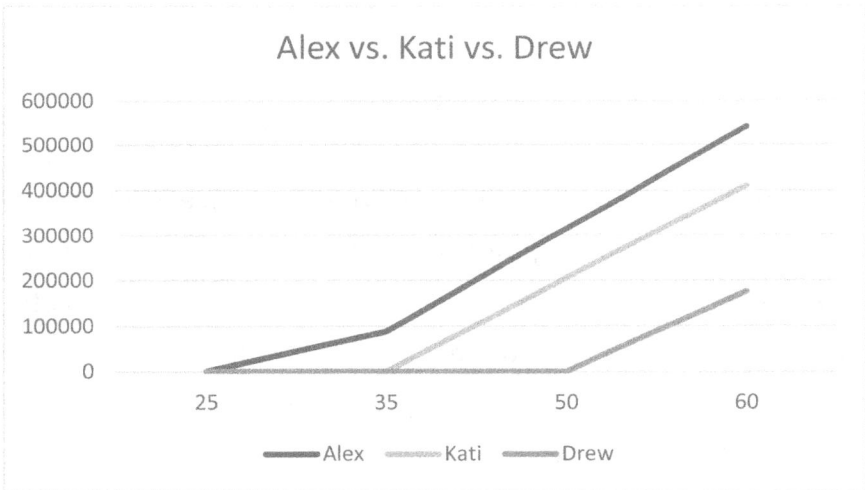

FIGURE 2. THE EARLIER YOU START INVESTING, THE BETTER OFF YOU'LL BE.

When it comes to investing, everyone likes to talk about the timing of the market, but the most important variable is time *in* the market. Starting early and remaining invested over an extended period of time is the recipe for success.

Save Early, Save Often

Compound interest has a powerful effect over time. The sooner you start saving for the future, the better off you'll be.

It's Never Too Late

One of the most common questions in my practice is whether it's too late to start planning for your future. I routinely coach folks in their fifties and sixties who ask if there's any hope for their retirement or if they will die at their desks. Although I'm not a fan of the classic retirement, I am a believer in the power and potential of planning your future. While planning later in life may limit your options, you also have the benefit of wisdom and experience, particularly when thinking about your legacy.

It may surprise you to realize what is truly possible if you put your mind to it. History is full of remarkable people who have achieved extraordinary things later in life.

Gladys Burrill ran a marathon (age 92)

Burrill earned recognition in the *Guinness Book of World Records* as the oldest female to complete a marathon. At 92 years old, she finished the race, which took place in Honolulu, in 9 hours, 53 minutes and 16 seconds. It was her fifth Honolulu finish in seven years.[4]

Julia Child started a cooking show (age 51)

While promoting her book, *Mastering the Art of French Cooking*, on a public TV station at the age of 50, Julia Child became a national sensation. Twenty-seven viewers wrote to the station, wanting to see more from this little-known talent. PBS produced three pilots, and then launched into production of *The French Chef*, which aired locally in 1962. The show went on to debut nationally the following year.[5]

Momofuku Ando launched a noodle sensation (age 61)

Ando was a Taiwanese-Japanese businessman who revolutionized the ramen noodle industry with his invention of Cup Noodles® in 1971 at the age of 61. This sparked the popularity of instant noodles, garnering a raving international fanbase.[6]

Peter Roget published a new type of book (age 73)

Although as a young man he began keeping lists of words, Roget didn't publish his thesaurus until the ripe old age of 73. To be fair, his collection of synonyms and antonyms was not the first one ever produced, but his was far better organized and more usable than those of his predecessors.[7]

Grandma Moses started painting (age 76)

One of the country's most famous painters began her artistic journey because of her love for embroidery. When arthritis crippled her hands, she found a new outlet in painting. Producing her first painting at the age of 76, her art eventually hung at the Museum of Modern Art in New York.[8]

Nelson Mandela began a political career (age 75)

After serving twenty-seven years in prison, Mandela was elected president of South Africa in 1993. He was the first non-white head of state in South Africa's history and the first to be elected in a fully representative democratic election following the dismantling of apartheid.[9]

Ray Kroc founded a burger empire (age 50)

From his car, Kroc was selling five-spindle milkshake mixers to drugstores and restaurants when he met Dick and Mac McDonald at their drive-up hamburger stand in Downey, California. Kroc opened the first McDonald's east of the Mississippi the following year.[10]

Teiichi Igarashi climbed a mountain (age 100)

In 1987, Teiichi Igarashi, a former lumberjack, became the first centenarian to climb Mt Fuji. It was his eleventh time to scale Japan's tallest mountain, and he attributed his success to eating raw eggs and receiving constant encouragement from his family and supporters.[11]

Every one of us has a legacy: you either intentionally define and nurture it throughout your life or it creates itself from your paths and choices. You have a legacy. Make it count.

Aim Before You Fire

Pulling the trigger on your financial game plan is relatively easy. The tricky part is defining your target and taking aim. What does a successful retirement look like? Is the classic notion of retirement a good fit for you, or do you prefer a more progressive, nuanced version? My perspective on retirement might seem contradictory. In Chapter One, I laid out all the ways in which the retirement landscape has changed from prior generations. In Chapter Two, I explained why the classic notion of retirement is flawed and why you need a purpose beyond your career and the extended unemployment called "retirement." Now I'm reinforcing the importance of investing money as early as possible so that compounding can work for you rather than against you.

While I certainly have concerns with the classic notion of retirement, I wholeheartedly support saving as an essential discipline to implement as soon as possible. What I reject is the magic number of dollars you can save to be set for life. It doesn't work that way. There are too many variables that are unique to your situation.

- Are you passionate and fulfilled by your work?
- Do you want to get out of the rat race before age fifty?
- Is your goal to travel and complete a bucket list while you are still young and active?
- Do you find fulfilment in your career and want to continue to engage in your industry as you age?
- Are you motivated by starting a ministry, charity, or community movement and being active in it throughout your career and retirement?

Clarifying your goals and priorities gives your life and your savings purpose and direction. You need to know where to aim.

Faucets and Buckets

Analogies and metaphors help me understand and teach new concepts. At Bluegrass Legacy Group, we use The Faucet and Bucket Income Strategy™ to illustrate the importance of effective financial planning and preparation. At the core of your roadmap are streams (or *faucets*) of income you turn on and off at various times. Similarly, you rely upon savings (or *buckets*) at different stages of your journey. Both enable you to live the full, legendary life you envision while also leaving your desired legacy.

Imagine your entire life as a journey. Along that journey you are going to get thirsty and will need reliable sources of clean water. Depending upon the stage of the journey, you might drink from a canteen, a water bottle, a water fountain, or a natural source you find along the way. Periodically, you're going to need to refill your containers so you'll have more water to drink later. In this metaphor, *faucets* represent streams of income to supply your daily needs. *Buckets* represent significant collections of resources you can use to supplement the flow of water from the faucets. That's how assets work throughout your life.

Here's a breakdown of the various elements:

- **Thirst (Needs).** Thirst represents your need to purchase goods, services, and experiences. Along your journey, your level of thirst will vary. Depending upon your life stage, you might also aim to quench the thirst of others (e.g., children or aging parents).
- **Water (Resources).** Water represents your ability to meet both your needs and the needs of those who depend on you. Typically it takes the form of money, but it could also include real assets, such as oil or precious metals.
- **Faucets (Income).** Faucets represent the various streams of water—i.e., the potential sources of income. These can include work, real estate, dividends, Social Security, pension, annuities, and business interests.
- **Buckets (Pools of Money).** Buckets represent your collection of water throughout your life. These include accounts (bank, brokerage, IRAs, 401(k)s, permanent insurance) or tangible assets (land, real estate, business interests). Those buckets, in

turn, can be used to supply your needs in place of or in partnership with the faucets.

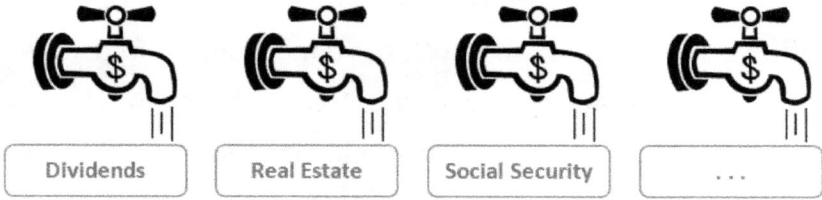

FIGURE 3. FAUCETS PROVIDE STREAMS OF MONEY YOU CAN ACCESS AS PART OF AN OVERALL INCOME STRATEGY THROUGHOUT YOUR LIFE.

The success of the Faucet and Bucket Income Strategy™ hinges on a few basic variables, including when to turn various faucets on and off, how to structure the buckets, and how to manage your thirst through discipline and careful rationing (i.e., budgeting).

Faucet and Bucket Scenario #1: Work Optional Lifestyle

A prudent investor throughout her lifetime, Avery always dreamed of one day investing back into herself as an entrepreneur. While pursuing her career, she relied heavily upon her salary as her primary stream of income (faucet) and diligently saved at least 15% annually to accumulate emergency cash (cash bucket). She also maintained a rental house (income bucket), a portfolio of dividend-paying stocks (income bucket), and an ample retirement savings (growth bucket). When Avery turned fifty-two, she retired from her full-time job to pursue her lifelong dream of opening a bubble tea stand. By leaning on her cash reserves and activating three income faucets (part-time consulting work, rental income, and stock dividend distributions), she was able to realize her dream of being her own boss.

FIGURE 4. BUCKETS COLLECT AND STORE RESOURCES OVER TIME. THEY ARE REBALANCED PERIODICALLY AND SUPPLEMENT THE FAUCETS AS NEEDED.

Faucet and Bucket Scenario #2: Navigating Recession

Garon joined the Army right after high school. He was careful to save and invest 10–12% of his pay every year. After two decades he retired from the Army at age forty with a military pension and three well-balanced buckets of investments. He then began a second career as a freelance musician. Because of the uncertainty in the music business, his financial planner recommended he rebalance the buckets and prioritize the cash and income buckets. Nine months into his journey as a starving artist, a recession hit. His long-term growth bucket suffered, but thanks to his conservative strategy with the other buckets, Garon was able to ride out the storm without an untimely withdrawal from his long-term resources.

Balancing the Buckets

Everyone's situation is different, complete with their own risks, concerns, opportunities, and goals. Correspondingly, the implementation of faucets and buckets will vary. However, common patterns will emerge, and the following parameters serve most people well:

- **Cash Bucket** (24 months of spending needs). Two year's worth of liquid savings should provide sufficient cash to ride out a recession without having to tap into your more long-term investments.
- **Income Bucket** (6 months of spending needs). This bucket is comprised of assets that generate a flow of income (real estate, bonds, dividend-paying equities, royalties, mineral rights, etc.). The income on these assets will vary, but the goal is to generate close to half of your spending needs through these income streams.
- **Growth Bucket** (remaining funds). This bucket includes long-term assets (raw land, growth stocks and index funds, business interests, etc.), which are less predictable but generate value and a higher potential return over a ten-year period or longer.

On a monthly basis, you spend distributions from your Cash Bucket. Quarterly or semiannually, you replenish your Cash Bucket through distributions from your Income Bucket. Annually or biannually, you harvest gains from the Growth

Bucket to replenish the Cash Bucket and purchase additional income assets.

You Can't Sail a Sinking Ship

Although a robust strategy for faucets and buckets is important, you can demolish this plan with poor budgetary discipline. Sailing fast is terrific, but if you're taking on water, you're going to sink. Accumulating assets with speed and momentum is gratifying and makes success easy to measure, but haphazard spending will thwart your goals. I've seen this same principle play out in my own journey of physical fitness. No amount of exercise can overcome an obsession with junk food. A personal trainer once told me, "Your health is 15% what you do in the gym and 85% what you do in the kitchen." You can't outwork a bad diet, and you can't out earn a runaway budget.

Delayed gratification affects everything from physical fitness to relationship building to financial health, and it is an important life skill. Perhaps John Stuart Mill said it best: "I have learned to seek my happiness by limiting my desires, rather than in attempting to satisfy them."[12] In the groundbreaking Stanford marshmallow experiment, researchers studied delayed gratification by offering children a choice between immediately receiving one small reward (a marshmallow) or a second reward (another marshmallow) if they were willing to wait.[13] In follow-up studies, the researchers found that those children who were able to wait longer tended to experience more success, including higher SAT scores,[14] educational attainment,[15] and even lower Body Mass Index (BMI).[16]

Financial success requires a thorough accounting of your expenditures and a willingness to stick to a spending plan. Yes, we're talking about the dreaded B-word: *Budget*. Returning to the nautical analogy, the effectiveness of your budget and corresponding cashflow means either having a tight ship that sails effortlessly through the water or a sketchy vessel that is taking on water, requiring frantic efforts to stay afloat. If you struggle to implement a budget (as many do), you may want to consider the following budgeting strategies:

Budget Strategy #1: 50/30/20

Every budget starts with defining spending categories and priorities. One well-known approach is the 50/30/20 system popularized by Elizabeth Warren in her book, *All Your Worth: The Ultimate Lifetime Money Plan*. [17] The essential tenets of the approach consist of allocating after-tax income into three high-level categories: 50% toward *needs* (housing, utilities, groceries, transportation, and minimal debt service), 30% toward *wants* (entertainment, dining out, and discretionary spending), and 20% toward *savings* (emergency fund, investing, extra debt payments).

The 50/30/20 system provides a useful framework for categorizing and tracking your spending. It gives you benchmarks in each category and corresponding subcategories to highlight areas of your spending which are out of recommended ranges. If you have more than half of your net income going toward necessities or over a third going toward discretionary wants, it will hinder your ability to save for your goals.

When to use 50/30/20. This strategy is most effective if you enjoy precision and desire a thorough accounting of cashflow.*

Budget Strategy #2: Manage the Mayhem

If tracking all your spending by category and subcategory isn't your idea of a good time, you may want to consider a more targeted approach to budgeting. Rather than tracking every element of your spending, identify the top three expense categories that are the greatest offenders for overspending. Common culprits include dining out, online shopping, recurring subscription services, and discretionary spending. Identify the three which are most prevalent for you, and focus your budgeting efforts on tracking, curtailing, and reallocating spending in these areas.

Targeting your budgeting efforts on a few select subcategories (typically discretionary spending or saving) is only viable if the other aspects of your budget are well established.

---

*If you believe this could be a viable budgeting approach for you, drop me an email at kyle@legendsdontretire.com and I'll be happy to send you a template.

This strategy assumes the bulk of your cashflow (income and expenses) are already mature and well managed.

When to use Manage the Mayhem. This approach is well suited when you have a healthy cashflow and a manageable debt load and would like to curb discretionary spending.

Budget Strategy #3: The Envelope System

Sometimes the simplest approach is the best. In the era of automated payments and debit card transactions, it is easy to become disconnected from our spending habits. In his bestseller, *The Total Money Makeover: A Proven Plan for Financial Fitness*,[18] financial guru Dave Ramsey promotes a cash-based system of categorized envelopes. By placing physical cash into labeled envelopes (e.g., groceries, entertainment, clothing) and refusing to spend money other than cash from an envelope, you adopt a highly disciplined budget.

Swiping or tapping a card is painless, and often it doesn't feel like we're spending real money. Something funny happens when you have to hand over cold hard cash. You think about your purchases more deeply. You force yourself to spend money consciously and constrain that spending to predetermined limits. In addition to strictly controlling your budget, this method has the added benefit of giving you a more direct connection to your spending habits and tendencies. While some find this technique works well for them in the long run, many utilize it as a temporary measure to gain control of their spending and put essential disciplines in place.

When to use the Envelope System. If you desire a closer connection with the flow of your money and a strict adherence to your intended budget, this seemingly old-fashioned method may be just what the financial doctor ordered.

Budget Strategy #4: Pay Yourself First

Most budgets begin with paying for your essential needs and then addressing your goals with the remaining excess. The Pay Yourself First strategy flips this classic mentality on its head. As with any budget, you start with your monthly net income. Next, rather than organizing your money and expenses into categories or percentages, you allocate funds to your savings targets and asset accumulation goals. Whatever is left is available for paying bills and other expenses.

Ultimately, any effort toward managing your cashflow is merely a means to an end. No one really wants a budget for its own sake. Instead, we seek to manage cash so we can pursue our goals and priorities. By intentionally focusing your budget on investing in yourself, you elevate the importance of achieving your goals. This strategy may result in making some very tough choices, forcing you to downsize your lifestyle and make difficult decisions, but it has the advantage of prioritizing your financial goals.

When to use Pay Yourself First. If you have low overhead or the willingness to reduce your fixed expenses, you may find this approach allows you to focus more intensely and work more aggressively toward your goals.

Budget Strategy #5: Fixed Plus Variable

My clients with variable income often object to budgeting. Whether due to commissions, bonuses, contract work, or overtime pay, there are many reasons your income might vary. Because variable income is unpredictable, think of your budget in terms of fixed and variable expenses. Fixed expenses constitute the baseline spending you require to meet your needs and maintain your life. These fixed expenses could even be managed by one of the previous four strategies. Variable expenses, on the other hand, are best handled through a collection of percentages. You can designate a set percentage of additional net income to saving, investing, extra debt payments, and discretionary spending. By utilizing percentages for these categories, it allows the variable portion of your budget to adapt to unpredictable income as it arrives.

Utilizing the Fixed Plus Variable strategy is certainly well suited for those with unpredictable income, but it also requires a lot of discipline to be successful. If the reliable portion of your income is lower than your fixed expenses, you may need to set aside significant portions of your variable income to make up the difference during the lean months.

When to use Fixed Plus Variable. This method is ideal if some or all of your income is unpredictable. Provided you have the discipline to carefully manage your fixed needs and allocate your variable income through percentages, this can be a powerful and flexible strategy.

Once you've selected a budgeting method (or combination of methods) that is right for you, you need to implement a system for tracking and accountability—anything from a basic template to a sophisticated, automated application. Fortunately, software packages and apps can easily simplify budgeting and cashflow management. Unfortunately, nothing trumps human nature. If you are unwilling to remain disciplined and stick to a budget, no amount of strategies and systems can save you. William Feather observes, "A budget tells us what we can't afford, but it doesn't keep us from buying it."[19] Curtailing spending isn't fun, but it is necessary.

Cashflow is King

Managing cashflow is essential to financial health. Try different budgeting strategies until you find what works.

You Need a Plan, Not an Arbitrary Number

Again, there is no magic number. Financial success is far more complex than merely accumulating a giant pile of money. As I've outlined throughout this chapter, each person is best served through a tailored financial plan incorporating several important qualities, including:

- the power of compound interest,
- a clearly defined set of prioritized goals,
- faucets of income and buckets of assets structured to meet your unique needs,
- a cashflow spending plan you are committed to keeping.

Sure, it's easier to accumulate $3 million because you heard that's what people need, but you don't need an arbitrary number. Instead, you need a roadmap uniquely crafted for your life goals, desired spending targets, appetite for work, legacy, and purpose.

Putting together a comprehensive financial plan is not trivial. Later chapters will lay out the essential elements of a custom life roadmap.

If you decide you don't want to embark upon this journey alone, drop me a line at kyle@legendsdontretire.com and let's have a conversation about your legacy goals.

Legendary Questions

1. Have you been saving with an arbitrary number in mind or with a financial plan tailored to your needs?

2. Do you currently have clarity regarding your current household spending and likely spending goals in the future?

3. What key decisions regarding income streams (faucets) and assets (buckets) do you need to make as part of your financial plan?

Chapter Four
Evolve, Don't Retire

Often when you think you're at the end of something, you're
at the beginning of something else.
—*Fred Rogers*

Heraclitus of Ephesus (c. 500 BCE) famously stated that "life is flux," and yet humans tend to handle change rather poorly. We prefer the status quo. We crave comfort and routine. This likely explains why retiring from one's career after investing thirty or forty years is often fraught with stress and uncertainty. I encourage my clients to embrace the change and consider a Work Optional Lifestyle. Rather than merely retiring *from* a career, I promote the importance of retiring *to* something else. That next stage of life could be volunteer work, a passion project, or a business you have always wanted to start. Evolving and finding fresh challenges will keep your mind stimulated. Otherwise, you might find yourself returning to work within months or even weeks of attempted retirement.

Legacy by the Decades

Executive coach, mentor, and author Bobb Biehl [1] has considerable insight into how our focus and motivations shift throughout our lives. Through coaching and mentoring thousands of executives one-on-one, he has developed a decade-by-decade framework that characterizes the key challenges and opportunities we face at each stage of life. The questions you grapple with in your twenties are starkly different than the ones in your fifties or sixties.

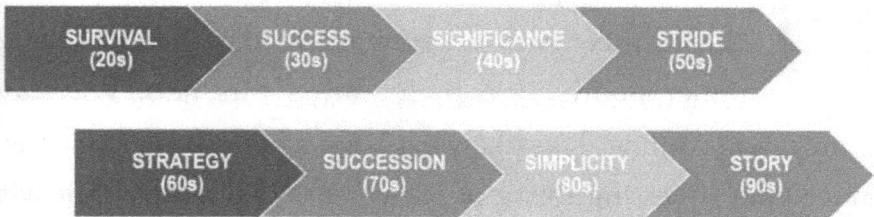

FIGURE 5. BOBB BIEHL DEFINES EACH DECADE WITH A PRIMARY THEME. I HAVE TAKEN THE LIBERTY TO SLIGHTLY REFRAME THE LAST TWO DECADES.

Bobb Biehl's profound insight into the human experience resonates with your own experiences and observations. With each passing decade, we confront new challenges. We build upon our prior successes, but this growth brings the next layer of obstacles, which challenge us to grow in new and different ways.

As I have digested Biehl's perspective and incorporated it into coaching hundreds of individuals and families through the financial planning process, I have gained clarity on how planning and living a legacy evolve over time. In the following descriptions, I've borrowed from and elaborated on Biehl's categories, and I've added fun adjectives (Roaring, Turbulent, Thrifty, etc.). For each stage, I've highlighted key considerations for planning goals and building and maintaining a legacy. The blend of his framework with my financial planning structure provides the building blocks for a roadmap to guide your financial growth and personal development. When seen as one part of your life's story, retiring is but one chapter. As the story unfolds, you have an opportunity to grow and mature into the next thrilling part of your adventure.

The Roaring 20s

I describe this as the "roaring" twenties because this is a time for fun, adventure, and taking risks. Although a bit messy at first, this is your chance for exploration and self-discovery. According to Biehl, your first decade of adulthood is about survival through grit and determination. You are stepping into the adult world of bills, career development, and rhythms and routines. At this point, you simply survive and learn to provide for your basic needs.

As you stumble through your twenties, it's important to define and establish core disciplines and sustainable habits.

Milestones in Your 20s

- Establish consistent income stream.
- Build cashflow discipline (spend less than you earn).
- Minimize/eliminate revolving debt.

- Commit to saving an increasing percentage of your income every year.

While the notion of legacy often feels like something only relevant at the end of your story, savvy planners aim to live a legacy, not just leave one behind.

Legacy Focus in Your 20s

- Find your rhythm and learn to manage money.
- Cut yourself some slack. Life is a marathon, not a sprint.

The Turbulent 30s

With one decade of adulthood under your belt, life in your thirties tends to be less chaotic, but now you fervently clamor to build a career, develop a social circle, and establish your place in the world. Many aspects of your life are still in flux. Biehl notes in this decade you tend to focus on achieving success and working feverishly to establish your place within your family, your career, and your community.

The most meaningful financial milestones of this decade center around security, peace of mind, and setting the stage to gain momentum in subsequent decades.

Milestones in Your 30s

- Establish an emergency fund covering three to six months of expenses.

- Establish a basic estate plan (wills and Powers of Attorney).
- Fully maximize your employer's savings plan and invest annually in a Roth IRA (if available).

As you consider a longer-term view of your legacy, your thirties provide an opportunity to begin investing in relationships which you may enjoy for the rest of your life.

Legacy Focus in Your 30s

- Find a mentor to guide you both personally and professionally.
- Become a mentor to someone else and start to pass along the lessons you've learned.
- Learn to balance your home and business schedule.
- Look for opportunities to increase your skills and long-term potential.

The Foundational 40s

Biehl defines this decade as a struggle for significance, wrestling with defining ourselves and our "single greatest strength"[2] and identifying what constitutes our "lifework."[3] Having emerged from our Turbulent Thirties and a preoccupation with success, we now struggle for significance because we have not yet found the comfort and consistency of our fifties.

By your forties, you've already carved out your career path, defined your social circle, and laid the groundwork for financial structures and disciplines—all foundational elements for personal and professional growth. Now life seems to pick up speed. Your career accelerates. Your family and social life expand. The demands on your schedule compound. Simply keeping all the plates spinning may seem overwhelming. At the same time, you already have the cornerstones to craft a meaningful legacy.

Milestones in Your 40s

- Increase your income (negotiate a raise and/or add additional streams, such as real estate or a side business).
- Build your team (tax professional, legal professional, financial coach—see Chapter Six, *You Need a Team*).
- Maximize your opportunities to save for the future.

Remember, while the notion of legacy often feels like something which is only relevant at the end of your story, savvy planners aim to live a legacy, not just leave one behind.

Legacy Focus in Your 40s

- Define your single greatest strength and lean into it.
- Discuss your parents' finances, estate plan, and legacy goals. You will ultimately be responsible to help them navigate their final life stages with grace.
- Revisit your estate plan and ensure it is long-term focused. Consider wealth transfer opportunities, tax impacts, and passing on a legacy for the next generation.

The Thrifty 50s

In your fifties, you may hit your stride with greater clarity about who you are and what success means to you, and you experience relief as someone with nothing to prove. Now more comfortable in your own skin, you embrace your identity and your beliefs within your professional and personal circles. This life stage is often characterized by greater confidence and a clearer sense of direction.

I describe this phase of life as "thrifty" because during this decade, most families invest a substantial percentage of their earnings. In prior decades, focused saving has been delayed due to mounting obligations (mortgage, education, children, parents). But the fifties enjoy higher income, less debt, and often an empty nest, making this decade a pivotal time for saving and investing.

Milestones in Your 50s

- Save aggressively.
- Solidify your plan for financial confidence (diversify income streams and tax strategy).
- Revisit your estate plan and update it to reflect your current strategy and mix of assets.
- Implement a plan for long-term care, which statistically will significantly drain your assets near the end of life.

Legacy Focus in Your 50s

- Increase your focus on physical, not just financial health.
- Become a mentor and continue to seek others who can mentor you.
- Create a "bucket list" of experiences and accomplishments that are important for you to achieve.

The Rocking 60s

According to Biehl, your sixties is a time of strategic thinking and the decade of greatest income and influence. While your natural energy may be decreasing, your strategic thinking is increasing. Bolstered by life experience and wisdom, you see the world more keenly than your younger self did. Your decisions are more measured, more informed, and more intentional.

Rather than losing momentum, your growth and influence can accelerate in your sixties. You succeed in your professional and social spheres with confidence and strength. You relish free time, investing freely in people and experiences that speak to your soul.

This exuberant pace of life starkly contrasts to how our parents and grandparents typically operated at the same age. While previous generations began to wind down at this point, today it is not uncommon in our sixties to earn more and grow more than in any previous decade. While your natural energy may be decreasing, your strategic energy is at its peak.

Milestones in Your 60s

- Plan out your retirement/Work Optional Lifestyle income plan (sources and timing for activating various faucets).
- Make decisions about Social Security and Medicare.
- Finalize your estate plan and wealth transfer strategy.

Legacy Focus in Your 60s

- Prioritize strategic thinking about your goals and your influence both personally and professionally.
- Define your identity in the absence of your career.
- Take steps to become more active in your family, your community, and any causes that you are passionate about.

The Transformational 70s

As you approach your seventh decade of life, a monumental transformation often occurs in your mindset and priorities, and you turn your attention toward succession planning. Motivated by a desire to influence, you shift your thoughts to successfully handing off your personal and professional legacy.

- Who will carry on your vocation and your values?
- What is the long-lasting effect of all your hard work and energy?
- How will you be remembered?

Your income and influence likely peaked during the past ten years, and coming to terms with that, slowing down, and defining a transfer of wealth to the next generation could be difficult. This transformation in your seventies, more than any other time, gives you the opportunity to pass along your wisdom and experience to enrich others.

Milestones in Your 70s

- Keep your estate plan updated, ensure you have selected the best executor, and communicate your intent.
- Coordinate your estate plan with charities and family members.
- Maximize opportunities to transfer your wealth in tax-efficient ways.
- Reduce the risk profile on your assets and income streams.

Legacy Focus in Your 70s

- Keep mentoring and investing in the lives of others, especially heirs of your estate.
- Document your memories and advice for the next generation.
- Find ways to hand off your priorities, not just your possessions.

The Influential 80s

According to Biehl's framework, the eighties are slippery in terms of health and finances. Health is unpredictable, and many peers pass away. While I understand Biehl's perspective, I also see this time as an opportunity to focus on influence and to prioritize simplicity.

In my eighties, I intend to do *less*. Less building, less hustling, and less striving. Instead, I'll redirect my energy toward giving back to the people and passions I care about the most. More giving and more mentoring. In your eighties, more than ever, it's important to streamline your life and finances. Simplify your assets, your schedule, and your priorities. In this decade, focus more intently on deepening your legacy's core elements.

Milestones in Your 80s

- Focus on your physical and mental health.
- Keep yourself stimulated with opportunities to learn, grow, and challenge your limits.
- Coordinate closely with trustees and trusted professionals.
- Identify anything from your bucket list you still want to achieve.

Legacy Focus in Your 80s

- Invest in people.
- Invest in your community.

The Gracious 90s

Closing in on a century of life, it's time to reflect on your life's story and embrace a mentality of abundance and gratitude. Biehl describes this phase with a theme of sleep. Although an accurate experience for many, it misses the significance of cultivating your story and facilitating a gracious hand-off to those people and organizations which you value.

So much of your mental and emotional well-being comes down to mindset. Now, more than ever, preserving a positive attitude is paramount. Continue to stimulate yourself with new challenges and new opportunities.

Milestones in Your 90s

- Keep learning and keep growing.
- Finish strong and finish well.

Legacy Focus in Your 90s

- Participate in the stewardship of your legacy by working closely with your family, organizations, and heirs to ensure the preservation of your values and intent in the assets and ideas you pass on.
- Share your wisdom often.

Change Is the Only Constant

Over time, your goals, priorities, and benchmarks for success naturally shift. At each phase of life, you should ask yourself different questions and stretch yourself in new ways. Growth throughout your life necessitates visualizing and pursuing a bigger and better future.

We typically define our annual goals or resolutions one year at a time, usually at the beginning of the calendar or fiscal year, but this approach is often too ambitious in the short term and too modest in the long run. Our eyes tend to be bigger than our stomachs as we commit to goals impossible to accomplish within twelve months while we overlook more realistic long-term goals. In Chapter Three, we explored compound interest as it relates to wealth accumulation. Interestingly, this same compounding effect applies to personal development as well.

Personal Growth Also Compounds

We tend to overestimate what is possible in one year and underestimate what we can accomplish in ten.

In his *New York Times* bestseller, *Atomic Habits,* James Clear describes the compounding effect of daily incremental improvement. "If you get one percent better each day for one year," he notes, "you'll end up thirty-seven times better by the time you're done."[4] Applying this principle to life goals across multiple decades creates endless possibilities.

By planning purposefully and living intentionally, your life could look dramatically different in twenty years. You could live anywhere in the world. You could speak a different language. You could have brand-new skills and capabilities. All the limitations in your career, finances, and social obligations could disappear if you commit to move beyond them.

Your current reality does not have to limit your remaining journey. The compounding effect of incremental change can radically redirect your trajectory. The choice is yours.

You don't have to retire. You can choose to evolve.

Legendary Questions

1. Reflecting on your previous decade, what are you most proud of accomplishing or overcoming?

2. At your current phase of life, what are your goals, milestones, and legacy focus?

3. Looking forward to the next life stage, what do you hope will be the most motivating or energizing?

Chapter Five
Legacy Should Be Lived, Not Just Left

Please think about your legacy because you are writing it every day.
—*Gary Vaynerchuk*

John and David Livingstone grew up in a Scottish family of seven children in the early 1800s. Determined to become wealthy, John set his mind and talents on commerce and making money, and he succeeded. Despite his material success, his legacy is overshadowed by that of his brother, David. While John vigorously pursued wealth, David committed himself to his faith and served as a missionary to remote parts of Africa. He dedicated his life to exploration, establishing trade routes, abolishing the African slave trade, and spreading his faith. His motto—now inscribed on his statue at Victoria Falls—was "Christianity, Commerce and Civilization." While his brother, John, was monetarily successful but had an arguably lesser influence, David was buried in Westminster Abbey with the inscription, "For thirty years his life was spent in an unwearied effort to evangelize."[1]

When we think of legacy, we often think of something left behind. While this is true, real legends live their legacy each day, one day at a time, allowing them the opportunity to experience the value they are creating and be a part of the impact they are making.

Standing Room Only

My father, Robert Gabhart, grew up on a tobacco and dairy farm in rural Kentucky. His day consisted of milking cows, going to school, practicing basketball, working on the farm, and completing his homework, and then he repeated the same routine the next day. Desperate to escape the monotony of farm life, he attended the University of Kentucky (Go Wildcats!), where he met my wonderful mother. After a brief courtship, they married in 1967. My father enlisted in the Army during the Vietnam War and my mother gave birth to my two sisters. Then in the late seventies, my family moved to Texas (fortuitously allowing me to be born a native Texan, a fact I never let my non-Texan family forget).

For the next three decades, my dad poured himself into the lives of others. He served as a gospel preacher, marriage and family counselor, summer youth camp director, soccer referee and commissioner, and he managed to coach nearly every sport I played. He gave selflessly of his time and talents to bless as many lives as he could.

After more than thirty years of ministry, he retired from preaching in 2007. He took a job with Child Protective Services for a few years to stay active until he stepped away from work entirely. Shortly after, he was diagnosed with Progressive Supranuclear Palsy (PSP), a rare brain disorder with similar symptoms to Parkinson's.

PSP is an aggressive disease that robs the afflicted of their emotional stability, motor control, and mental acuity in less than a decade. In my father's case, he quickly lost the ability to drive and to walk without assistance. He progressed rapidly from a walker to a weighted walker, and ultimately he was confined to a wheelchair. Soon after, he required a catheter and a feeding tube. In less than six years, all his faculties were ripped away from him.

On July 29, 2018, Robert Gabhart passed away due to PSP complications. Although he had invested in the lives of others for most of his life, it had been a long time since he had been able to serve. He hadn't been in the pulpit in eleven years. He hadn't even been able to contribute meaningfully to a relationship during the last five years of his life. As we planned the memorial service, we couldn't help but wonder—who would attend after all this time?

It was raining heavily the morning of August 11, and while we had received a generous outpouring of support since our father's death, we wondered who would venture out. As my sisters and I were texting that morning, one of them shared Harry Truman's quip about weather being the great equalizer in death: "It doesn't matter how big a ranch you own or how many cows you brand, the size of your funeral is still gonna depend on the weather."[2]

With more than a decade separating our father from the lives he had so intentionally blessed, who would still remember? How many would actually show up?

It was standing room–only at Lake Cities Church in Trophy Club, TX. On that miserable rainy morning, more than 300 people braved the elements to pay their respects. Plans were changed, vacations were canceled, and people traveled from six states to celebrate the life of Robert Gabhart.

Person after person shared stories of how our father had influenced their families and changed the trajectory of their lives. They described his profound effect on them and their families twelve years ago, fifteen years ago, even twenty-five years ago. The significant mark he left on each soul compelled them to honor his memory.

I learned the true meaning of the word *legacy* that day.

You Have a Story to Live

By shifting our perspective from *leaving* a legacy to *living* a legacy, we seize the opportunity to take an active role in the story we tell, the lives we touch, and the indelible impact we make. That legacy impact can be lived out through three primary avenues: time, treasure, and talents.

Living a Legacy with Your Time

If you are passionate about a particular cause, such as prison ministry or equipping women escaping abusive relationships,* what is more meaningful for you: leaving a pile of money to the cause after your death, or rolling up your sleeves to become a part of the change you want to see? By being actively involved, you are living your values. You can positively affect the world, sharing your vision and motivating others to do the same. Furthermore, living your values and writing your legacy story throughout your life helps you define your identity apart from your career.

Living a Legacy with Your Treasure

Giving back through monetary investment might seem straightforward, but there's more complexity here than meets the eye. Different giving strategies carry pros and cons for the donor as well as the organization receiving the support. Strategies you may want to consider include:

- Establishing a Donor Advised Fund (DAF)
- Establishing a family foundation
- Consolidating charitable gifts into a single year to offset income (sometimes described as "bunching" gifts)
- Utilizing Charitable Remainder Trust (CRT) structures to meet current personal needs and future charitable goals

---

*Unlocked Ministries does fantastic work empowering women as they exit abusive relationships. https://www.unlockedministries.com.

- Utilizing Charitable Lead Trust (CLT) structures to meet current charitable goals and future personal goals
- Giving sustained gifts over time instead of one-time gifts
- Utilizing tax benefits of Qualified Charitable Distributions (QCD) directly out of a retirement account
- Gifting highly appreciated stocks, bonds, or other appreciated assets (real estate, business interests, etc.)

Each of these approaches can significantly affect your tax strategy and estate plan. Thorough planning will help you determine ways to give that will not only be in your best interest but will also produce the most advantageous results for the cause or organization who receives your gifts. In the next chapter, we'll discuss the importance of forming a team to partner with you in crafting a strategy tailored to your unique situation.

Living a Legacy with Your Talents

Undoubtedly, you have natural talent or a cultivated skillset that has served you well. You might currently use these gifts within a hobby or your professional life. It could be a gift for public speaking, a knack for working with your hands, or a competency around process and organization. Whatever your talents, you can apply them to a cause you care about or a mark you want to leave on the next generation. Consider how you can put your talents to work in writing your legacy now while you can still see the fruits of your investment.

When the time comes to slow down and shift into a Work Optional Lifestyle, you can further engage in those things you care most about, providing a catalyst for service to something greater than yourself.

Make a Difference

Applying your time, treasure, and talents toward causes you care about is an essential part of defining a legacy.

Questions to Ask

Martha Duesterhoft, a partner with PeopleResults, encourages asking yourself several probing questions to discover who you are outside your vocation.

- What does success look like for me? (Define a vision for success.)
- What do I want to be known for? (Identify themes for your life.)
- What are my top three values? (Define your beliefs and priorities.)
- Am I living in a way that reflects those values? (Consider how you spend your time and talents.)

All of this speaks to the subject of the legacy you are living "one day at a time, one person at a time, over a lifetime."[3]

Philanthropy advisor Dawn Franks beautifully describes legacy as a story told throughout our lives: "The very nature of legacy is storytelling. Our life stories are like a river that draws you along on its current. While you can't quite see beyond the bend, looking back is rich with story."[4]

Know Thyself

Uncovering who you are as distinct from what you do is an instrumental part of defining your legacy.

The Secret to Living Is Giving

Each of us will give our lives to something. We give our time, money, energy, and talents each day. The culmination of these daily choices produces the sum of the life we live and the memories we create.

- Do we give ourselves to developing a company or a community?
- Do we give ourselves to creating a following or creating a family?

- Do we give ourselves to pursuing money or pursuing a mission?

Where you choose to invest your time and talents speaks volumes about your values and priorities.

World-renowned motivational speaker, Tony Robbins, coined a phrase that is at the heart of a meaningful life: "The secret to living is giving." He explains:

> Giving back and learning how to make an impact on others provides that meaning because it makes life about something much larger than ourselves. It fulfills our essential human need to feel significant as well as the human need to contribute. When we help others, we grow in our personal lives and make progress toward unlocking an extraordinary life. We break out of our limiting beliefs about how much good one person can do in the world and see firsthand that even the smallest acts of kindness can transform lives.[5]

It's those "smallest acts of kindness" that we so often dismiss as insignificant. We imagine only large amounts of money or power make a difference. Celebrating grand gestures is important, but the small, consistent investments we make in others compound over a lifetime and ripple throughout generations.

Eight Simple Acts of Kindness to Live a Legacy

1. Donate school supplies.
2. Volunteer at a local food pantry.
3. Become a mentor.
4. Donate clothing to a shelter or children's home.
5. Smile. It's infectious.
6. Tip generously.
7. Donate blood.
8. Pick up trash.

The possibilities are endless. Consider the difference you want to make in the lives you encounter and the communities you enjoy. Look around your circles of influence and creatively imagine the many ways you can invest in others, actively participating in living your legacy.

Edward Everett Hale was a nineteenth-century American Unitarian minister and author. A literary child prodigy, Hale graduated from Boston Latin School and enrolled in Harvard at thirteen. He lived and worked in Boston, Massachusetts, and won critical acclaim for his short stories and poetry.[6] In one particularly inspirational passage, he writes about the power and potential within each of us to make a mark on the people and the passions we hold most dear. Hale writes,

> I'm only one,
> but I am one.
> I can't do everything,

but I can do something.
What I can do,
I ought to do.
And what I ought to do,
by the grace of God
I will do.[7]

Legendary Questions

1. Looking back over your life, what causes, organizations, values, or passions have most energized you?

2. What opportunities exist right now to utilize your time, treasure, or talents in giving to your family, your community, or an organization you are passionate about?

3. Casting your vision forward, what future contribution do you hope to make within your spheres of influence?

Chapter Six
The Anti-Retirement Plan

In preparing for battle, I have always found that plans are useless,
but planning is indispensable.
—*Dwight D. Eisenhower*

I n the spring of 1981, Carl McCunn, a thirty-four-year-old wildlife photographer, was flown into a desolate part of northern Alaska to photograph the natural beauty and mysteries of the tundra. He planned extensively in preparation for this five-month adventure. He took along five hundred rolls of film, several firearms, and 1,400 pounds of provisions.[1] As the months passed, the words in his diary changed from wonder and fascination to despair. In August he wrote, "I think I should have used more foresight about arranging my departure. I'll soon find out." In November he died in a nameless valley, by an insignificant lake, 225 miles northeast of Fairbanks. A subsequent investigation revealed that though he had carefully planned and prepared for his trip, he had failed to plan for his departure. [2]

McCunn's tragedy highlights a common problem inherent in financial planning. Extensive effort is made to save, accumulate assets, and prepare to leave the workforce, but very little thought is given to planning for the post-retirement years. How will assets translate into reliable income streams? How will you remain engaged and stimulated in the absence of a day job? How will the plan survive against the ravages of inflation and rising medical costs over multiple decades?

Building a nest egg is an important part of any successful financial plan, but without a thoughtful strategy to navigate the subsequent years, you could find yourself lost in the wilderness without a means of escape.

Reaching the Summit Isn't Enough

Ever since Sir Edmund Hillary and Tenzing Norgay became the first confirmed climbers to reach the summit of Mount Everest in 1953, scaling the summit has become a bucket list achievement for adrenaline junkies around the world.

Climbing Everest is not without its hazards. Nearly every year since 1969, someone has died trying to conquer the world's highest peak.[3] Contrary to popular belief, the ascent is not the most dangerous part of the journey.

A study released by the *British Medical Journal* in 2008 found 56% of deaths on Everest occurred during descent from the summit with another 17% attributed to those who turned back after their final ascent.[4] That means 73% of all deaths among climbers occurred while *descending* the mountain. The climb isn't what you have to worry about; the real danger lies in the return.

Everest climber and exercise psychologist Shaunna Burke describes the problem faced by many climbers: "At that altitude, it takes everything to put one foot in front of the other. If you haven't judged how much gas you have left in the tank, then you can't make it down. That's why some climbers sit down and don't get back up."[5]

Climbing Mount Everest provides a compelling parallel for goal setting and life planning. Just as most deaths occur while descending the mountain, most financial plans unravel during the distribution phase of retirement. Advance decisions regarding the timing of income streams (the faucets from Chapter 3), balancing your assets across multiple categories (the buckets), navigating tax considerations, and paying for healthcare must be considered far ahead of your actual retirement. We focus so much energy on reaching the goal, which is often a set number of assets or net worth, that we lose sight of planning our descent of the proverbial mountain.

Reaching your goal is only half the story. It's the easier and more glamourous half, and its achievement is exhilarating. But it leaves too many unanswered questions. In the absence of a thoroughly planned and executed second half, your magical adventure could turn into a horrific tragedy.

Planning Is a Process

Financial planners are notorious for printing large volumes of paper with impressive charts and stuffing them into fancy binders as if these advisors were compensated by the pound. While these formalized deliverables look impressive and give the feeling of value, they are outdated the moment they are printed.

Future-oriented plans for your life and your money attempt to assess how events will transpire over many years. In the absence of a Magic 8 Ball, advisors must make a slew of assumptions about inflation, interest rates, tax rules, returns by asset class, distribution strategies, and economic cycles. Then they fold all these considerations into a comprehensive plan; unfortunately, the relevance of that plan tends to dissolve over time.

The markets change. Politics change. Tax rules change. Interest rates change. Industries change. Your goals and priorities change.

A *plan* is a physical, tangible construct that is static by nature. It represents one perspective during a single point in time.

Planning is a process. It's a dynamic approach that adapts to ongoing challenges and obstacles.

Defining FINANCIAL PLANNING

A dynamic process of goal setting, priority alignment, and cashflow management to optimize your life and financial resources.

Having a plan is vastly superior to not having one. But even the most well-crafted plan merely represents a single approach created with a set of reasonable assumptions. It remains valid until those assumptions change, and once that occurs, the plan must adapt to the new reality. Over a decade or longer, there are a lot of potential changes to accommodate.

Your life is dynamic. This world is dynamic. Your planning needs to be dynamic as well. But you don't need to embark upon this endeavor alone.

You Need a Team

Bill Gates needed Steve Balmer. Steve Jobs needed Steve Wozniak (what is it with tech giants named Steve?). Michael Jordan needed Scottie Pippen, Tim Grover, and Phil Jackson. Teamwork is essential in business and sports. However intelligent, experienced, or capable you may be, you need a team. You can't know everything, and you can't see your life from every perspective. If you want to build a comprehensive roadmap which stewards your legacy well, you need a team of professionals to provide you with wise counsel.

Team Member #1: Tax & Accounting

Ratified in 1913, the Sixteenth Amendment created a federal income tax for the United States. The initial code contained a whopping four pages of forms and instructions. Those were the good old days. The most recent update to the Internal Revenue Code (June 23, 2022) is 6871 words in length.[6] When you include the federal tax regulations and supplemental official tax guidance, the number of pages exceeds seventy thousand. The sheer volume of information is overwhelming. You need a seasoned tax and accounting expert to navigate and correctly apply the rules to your unique situation

HA! Legends Learn to Laugh

A fine is a tax for doing wrong.
A tax is a fine for doing well.

The right accountant will help you strategize business structure, asset depreciation, and achieve tax efficiency. They will also help you to implement effective accounting and control processes to ensure you are correctly tracking money movement and significant transactions throughout the year.

Tips for finding the right tax & accounting professional. Find an individual (or ideally a team) who will focus on tax strategy and collaborate with the rest of your team to develop a comprehensive approach. Plenty of competent tax professionals will operate as order takers, plugging your data into forms and filing them for you. You don't need a tax filer; you need a strategic tax partner.

Team Member #2: Legal

You can balance your own books and file your own taxes. You shouldn't, but you can. In the legal world, however, attempting to self-educate and provide your own legal counsel is a recipe for disaster. Online legal document services, such as LegalZoom, are deceptively simple. You can't enter information into a template and assume you're safe. There's too much at risk.

HA! — **Legends Learn to Laugh**

Q: Why won't sharks attack lawyers?
A: Professional courtesy.

Depending upon your situation, you may need multiple attorneys on your team. Typical examples include the following:

- **Business Formation & Contracts**. If you have a business or are a partner in a business, a trusted attorney who specializes in this area of law is an essential part of your team.

- **Estate Planning Attorney.** Everyone has an estate. Everyone knows they should protect this estate, but not everyone does. Crafting a will, powers of attorney (POA), and trusts (when appropriate) are a key part of any comprehensive plan.
- **Outside General Counsel.** You may find you have a variety of specialized legal needs (e.g., copyright & intellectual property, real estate, tax). It's helpful to have a generalist who can answer basic legal questions and direct you to a specialist when needed.

Tips for finding the right legal professionals. An attorney is often called a counselor. Find someone (or ideally a team) to counsel you through legal matters as the complexity of your life, business, and estate increases. Many firms will have several areas of expertise, so you may be able to check several boxes with a single relationship.

Team Member #3: Insurance

Insurance isn't glamorous, but it is valuable. Insurance allows you to transfer risk to a third party, and a good insurance broker will help you understand your personal and professional risk exposures. They will help you wisely balance premium, risk, and coverage. As your business and real estate interests become more complicated, the importance of insurance increases accordingly.

HA!

Legends Learn to Laugh

Needing insurance is like needing a parachute. If it isn't there the first time, chances are you won't be needing it again.

Certain types of life insurance policies can aid your estate plan later in life. Tax-advantaged income, efficient wealth transfer, and long-term care planning are all achievable through effective utilization of life insurance policies.

Tips for finding the right insurance professional. Insurance agents tend to get a bad rap, but there are some truly consultative professionals out there. In your search, look for an independent broker who works with multiple carriers to find your best coverage. Your representative should also educate you about risk and coverage, helping you better understand the specific policies you may need to mitigate all your risks.

Team Member #4: Banking

For our parents and grandparents, having the right banker was a game-changer. Bankers were the power brokers who guided their clients through a sea of professionals and strategies to solve their financial challenges. Times have changed. In an era where you can handle all your banking needs online or at the drive-through ATM, recognizing the importance of a consultative banker on your team can be challenging.

HA!

Legends Learn to Laugh

If bankers are so good with numbers, why do they have five windows and only two tellers?

A good banker can help you utilize other people's money to strategically grow your assets. Lending options, lines of credit, and the tangled world of the Small Business Administration (SBA) are all areas a banking partner can help you navigate.

Tips for finding the right banking professional. Look for a consultative banker who asks you about your strategy and goals. You need someone who seeks to understand how your cashflow and spending patterns change throughout the year, then offers creative approaches to your cashflow, cash reserves, and lending needs.

Team Member #5: Financial Advisor

Traditionally, financial advisors are associated with stockbrokers and stock pickers, but investment advice is just one of many services a competent financial advisor provides. Any robot can build you a portfolio (and many robo-advisors are ready to do so), and the increasing commoditization of the investment world makes constructing a well-balanced portfolio easy. Beyond investment counseling, a skilled financial advisor will also guide your entire team in making decisions. Next-generation financial advisors are the thread that ties the other members of the team together.

HA!

Legends Learn to Laugh

Money isn't everything.
But it certainly keeps the kids in touch.

Everyone on your professional team has knowledge and skills in a specific, specialized field. Financial advisors operate as a jack-of-all-trades to guide you in the development and execution of a comprehensive life plan. Indeed, a financial advisor touches all aspects of your world and provides context and strategic direction to the tactical guidance provided by the other members of the team. Your advisor will collaborate with you to integrate their advice into a cohesive strategy and hold you accountable to implementing that strategy throughout your life.

Tips for finding the right financial professional. This one's easy. Just hire Bluegrass Legacy Group. Problem solved. Seriously though, you need a financial advisory team who will help you uncover your priorities and articulate your goals. Look for an advisor who will work with you and your family to define and steward your legacy while you are still able to take an active role.

> ## Teamwork Makes the Dream Work
>
> If you want to go fast, go alone.
> If you want to go far, go together.
>   — African Proverb

Our world is complex. You and your family need someone in your corner to advise you in the tax, legal, insurance, and banking realms. To integrate all of this, you need a trusted financial advisor. As we say around our office, "Teamwork makes the dream work!"

Diversification* Is Your Friend

In 1952, American economist Harry Markowitz published his Modern Portfolio Theory (MPT)[7] for which he would later be awarded a Nobel Prize.[8] Among other things, MPT espouses the importance of diversifying your investments across different industries, regions, and investment types in order to balance risk and reward while also reducing the volatility of the portfolio. Portfolio diversification is important, but there are three other types of diversification even more crucial for the success of a

---

* Diversification does not guarantee a profit or protect against a loss in a declining market. It is a method used to help manage investment risk.

well-balanced financial plan: diversified assets, diversified income, and a diversified tax strategy.

Diversify Your Assets

Yes, you should diversify your investment portfolio. But well-diversified investments are only one type of asset. Ultimately you should aim to accumulate more than just stocks and bonds to have a truly diverse asset portfolio. Different types of assets include:

- Art & collectibles
- Business interests
- Cash and cash equivalents
- Diversified investment portfolio
- Real estate*
- Vehicles and equipment

You don't necessarily need to accumulate assets in every category, but diversifying your mix of assets across multiple categories helps provide you with greater financial confidence.

Diversify Your Income

One stream of income is certainly preferable to no income, but it does come with significant risk. With only one income source, you have limited options to adapt and respond to inevitable

---

*Direct real estate ownership has a lot of tax advantages as long as you are willing to deal with the associated costs and hassles. For those who merely want the asset and income diversification, you can gain indirect access to real estate through real estate investment trusts (REITs) or syndications.

challenges. Furthermore, if anything compromises your sole income stream, you have nothing to fall back on. That's why I encourage my clients to develop multiple avenues for income both during the accumulation phase of life (i.e., typical working years) as well as the distribution phase (retirement/Work Optional). Different streams of income include the following:

- Annuities
- Compensation for work (contract or salary)
- Dividends from business
- Dividends from investment portfolio
- Interest income
- Pension
- Rental income
- Royalties
- Social Security

Again, developing all of these isn't necessary, but every additional income stream improves the resilience of your financial game plan.

Diversify Your Tax Strategy

The tax code is a moving target. It evolves every few years with new rules, additional interpretations, and expanded regulations. To maximize your benefits, your portfolio should reflect a diversified tax strategy.

There are three primary tax categories to consider:

1. **Pre-tax assets** (a.k.a. tax-deferred). This category refers to assets funded through untaxed compensation. These assets remain sheltered from tax until they are accessed (typically many years in the future). When the money is retrieved, it is treated as income and taxed accordingly. The most common examples are a 401(k) or traditional Individual Retirement Account (IRA). Other pre-tax assets include 403(b), 457, profit-sharing plan, cash balance plan, Thrift Savings Plan (TSP), Savings Incentive Match Plan for Employees (SIMPLE) IRA, and Simplified Employee Pension Plan (SEP) IRA.

2. **Post-tax assets.** When you use previously taxed income to acquire assets, those investments are considered post-tax. Unlike pre-tax assets, already-taxed investments are subject to capital gains tax with any taxable event (sale, dividend, or distribution). Generally speaking, capital gains tax is significantly preferable to income tax. Post-tax assets include bank and brokerage accounts, precious metals, cryptocurrency, art and collectibles, real estate, vehicles, business interests, and anything else of value you purchase with previously taxed income.

3. **Tax "free" assets.** My economics professor taught me "There is no free lunch." Everything has a price. Nothing is truly free. The same is true with this asset category. There are a handful of assets that, if you navigate the rules correctly, can avoid certain categories of tax entirely. Roth 401(k) and Roth IRA

accounts are funded with post-tax dollars, but their growth is sheltered from tax. Life Insurance Retirement Plan (LIRP) distributions and life insurance beneficiary distributions are generally tax-free. Interest distributed from municipal bonds avoids federal income tax but is still subject to state income tax.

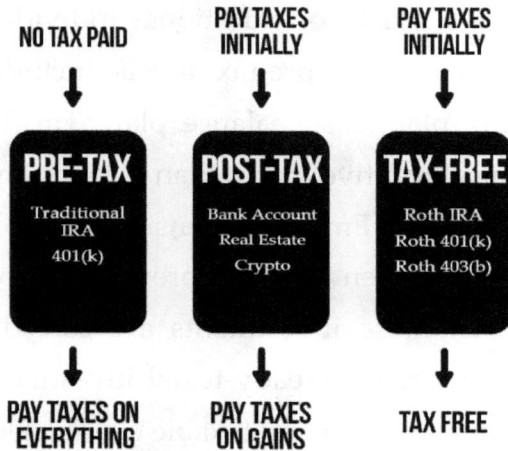

NO TAX PAID	PAY TAXES INITIALLY	PAY TAXES INITIALLY
↓	↓	↓
PRE-TAX	**POST-TAX**	**TAX-FREE**
Traditional IRA 401(k)	Bank Account Real Estate Crypto	Roth IRA Roth 401(k) Roth 403(b)
↓	↓	↓
PAY TAXES ON EVERYTHING	PAY TAXES ON GAINS	TAX FREE

FIGURE 6. DIVERSIFYING YOUR TAX STRATEGY PROVIDES YOU WITH FLEXIBILITY IN THE FUTURE SO YOU CAN ADAPT TO AN EVER-CHANGING TAX LANDSCAPE.

By funding all three asset categories, you will have maximum flexibility to adapt to the inevitably shifting tax landscape. In any given year, you'll be positioned to draw from each category as needed to produce the optimum balance between income and tax.

Planning the Summit

Yankees catcher and king of the one-liners Yogi Berra once famously said, "If you don't know where you are going, you'll end up someplace else."[9] Comprehensive financial planning is the key to intentional living. It lends clarity and direction by embracing what Stephen Covey identifies as the second of seven habits to success: "Begin with the End in Mind."[10] Once you know your target, you can work backward to define the steps necessary to achieve it.

Key Considerations during the Accumulation Phase

- **Cashflow is King.** Focus on increasing your income streams (both quality and quantity) while responsibly managing your spending. Healthy and sustainable cashflow is paramount.

- **Determine and Diversify**. Decide on your asset accumulation target. Whether you choose a classic retirement scenario or a more progressive Work Optional approach, the fundamentals are the same: diverse income streams, conservative spending targets, and realistic expectations about inflation, taxes, and healthcare needs over time.

- **Bridging the Preretirement Age Gap**. At the time of this writing, there are multiple investment vehicles tethered to age 59.5 (mostly coming from the pre-tax asset list described earlier). Social Security benefits begin at age sixty-two or later and Medicare coverage begins at age sixty-five. Anyone aiming to achieve a Work Optional Lifestyle prior to their sixties will need more creative income streams than a cash stockpile in their 401(k). Multiple income streams, substantial post-tax assets, and advanced distributions strategies* are all part of a carefully constructed plan.

- **Living on Purpose.** Legacy is meant to be lived, not just left. Find your passion. Identify something bigger than yourself. Roll up your sleeves and get involved in shaping your legacy throughout your remaining years.

Planning the Descent

Zig Ziglar once said, "It's not where you start that matters. It's where you finish that counts." [11] If financial planning was important during the asset accumulation phase of your life, it is even more important to effectively navigate during the distribution phase. Haphazardly managing the distribution of your assets and the timing of your income streams can wreck even the most robust nest egg.

Key Considerations during the Distribution Phase

- **Cash reserves are a necessity**. During your accumulation phase, you need a buffer of cash to cover several months' expenses. As you transition into the distribution phase of

---

*There are a variety of advanced distribution strategies for bridging the pre-retirement age gap which are beyond the scope of this text. Examples include Rule of 55, Substantially Equal Periodic Payments (SEPP) via Rule72(t), Roth distribution ladder, Roth conversion ladder, Life Insurance Retirement Plan (LIRP), and more.

your journey, you'll want cash and cash equivalents to supply you for at least two years. By establishing two to three years of cash, you are insulated from the pain of bear markets and recessions. This cash bucket (Chapter 3) provides the necessary resources to weather an economic storm.

- **Carefully plan distributions.** Distributing assets from your investment accounts or realizing income from business and real estate interests carries tax implications. Coordination with your team of advisors is crucial. The source of the distribution, the length of time you've owned the asset, and the other facets of your tax strategy are all relevant factors.

- **Manage risk over time**. As you age, it's important to manage the risk of your asset portfolio. You can improve the consistency and predictability of your balance sheet by selling more aggressive, volatile assets (high growth stocks, crypto, most commodities, speculative real estate) in favor of more conservative, stable ones (cash, gold, municipal bonds, dividend-paying investments). This is sometimes referred to as a "glide path" because you glide over time toward a more predictable landing.

- **Prioritize healthcare.** As you age, you need to prioritize healthcare and eventually engage in Long-Term Care planning (LTC)*. Healthcare continues to be one of the most

---

*Funding your LTC plan can take many forms. LTC insurance is one popular approach, but it becomes more expensive the longer you wait to start the policy. Carving out dedicated assets to cover LTC costs is another common

significant expenses later in life. The most current estimates predict the average retiree will allocate 15% of their annual spending to healthcare-related expenses.[12] Later in life, LTC planning is an even greater concern. According to the Department of Health and Human Services, someone turning sixty-five in 2022 has a 70% likelihood of needing long-term care.[13] Healthcare expenses are unavoidable.

- **Live with passion and purpose**. Stewarding your legacy means determining the impression you want to make on the people around you. Choosing how you will invest your time, treasure, and talents are some of the most important decisions you'll make. Set your mind every day on building your legacy and investing in the people and causes you care for the most. Everything else is secondary.

Carl McNunn had a plan for the first half of his journey, but successful mountain climbers plan for more than just the reaching the summit. With careful planning for both the ascent (asset accumulation phase) and descent (asset distribution phase) of your financial journey, you don't have to be a statistic. By assembling a strong team of advisors and approaching your planning as a dynamic, on-going process, you can write the legacy you envision.

---

strategy. Finally, many families rely upon in-home care from family members as an early step in their LTC plan.

Legendary Questions

1. Which members of your advisory team (tax/accounting, legal, insurance, banking/lending, financial planning) already exist, and what gaps do you need to fill?

2. How can you further diversify your assets, your income, or your tax strategy?

3. How can you ensure a successful ascent (wealth accumulation) and descent (wealth distribution) in your life?

Chapter Seven
A Plan in Motion

If you could kick the person in the pants responsible for most of
your trouble, you wouldn't sit for a month.
—*Theodore Roosevelt*

I n *The Empire Strikes Back,* Master Yoda trains Luke Skywalker to harness the power of The Force. After learning to move stones with his mind, Luke's next feat is to lift his X-wing fighter from the swamp.

Luke: Master, moving stones around is one thing. This is totally different.

Yoda: No! No different! Only different in your mind. You must unlearn what you have learned.

Luke: All right, I'll give it a try.

Yoda: No! Try not. Do. Or do not. There is no try.[1]

When it comes to your financial roadmap, you can't "try it" or hope things will work out. Trying implies it may not happen, and hope is not a strategy. You need to make a commitment, gather your courage, and take action to chart the path for your future.

Go BIG

One of my mentors, Lee Brower, begins every speech and every meeting with what he calls Go BIG (Begin in Gratitude). This mindset has profoundly influenced my personal and professional life. My family established "Go BIG" at the dinner table, and we begin each meal by sharing something we are grateful for. The effect is extraordinary. I've implemented this same practice for team meetings and client appointments. In my experience, starting with a positive mindset has been transformative, encouraging, energizing, and rewarding.

That's great, Kyle, but what does that have to do with legacy planning? Gratitude allows you to dream about the future and casts a vision for what is possible. International bestselling author, Melody Beattie, expresses the power of gratitude beautifully.

> Gratitude unlocks the fullness of life. It turns what we have into enough, and more. It turns denial into acceptance, chaos to order, confusion to clarity. . . . It turns problems into gifts, failures into successes, the unexpected into perfect timing, and mistakes into important events . . . . Gratitude makes sense of our past, brings peace for today, and creates a vision for tomorrow.[2]

Gratitude sets the tone, frames your perspective, and cultivates a mindset of abundance. When you begin with gratitude, your planning and vision take an entirely different trajectory.

As you embark upon the definition and implementation of your financial roadmap, begin with gratitude.

Plan around Your Passion

You are not your job. You are not your portfolio. If you retired tomorrow or sold your business, what would you do next? Is your identity defined by what you do or who you are? Genuine success starts by defining yourself outside the context of work (see Chapter 5).

If you're still struggling to find your passion, or what Bobb Biehl calls your "lifework," Biehl recommends asking yourself these questions:[3]

- What would you enjoy doing the rest of your life?
- What makes you weep or pound the table?
- Of all the things you do well, what do you do the very best?
- What difference do I want to make before I die?

Once you understand what motivates and energizes you, begin setting goals and milestones accordingly. You'll want to elaborate this goal framework as a set of progressive milestones (see Chapter 4 on the evolution of legacy by the decades).

1. **Set the Vision.** Start by setting a high-level, aspirational vision for the next twenty years.

   - What will be true of your life at this point?
   - What are your professional and/or financial targets?
   - How would you characterize your family and personal status?
   - Is there anything significant you hope to achieve?

2. **Define a Key Milestone.** Set a milestone at the halfway mark.

   - What makes achieving your personal vision possible?
   - What makes achieving your professional and financial vision possible?
   - How will you know if you are on track to achieving the ultimate vision?

3. **Define an Incremental Milestone.** Set a closer milestone at three to five years.*

   - What needs to occur for you to be satisfied with your personal progress?
   - What needs to occur for you to be satisfied with your professional progress?

---

*These questions are inspired by "The Dan Sullivan Question," crafted by Dan Sullivan of Strategic Coach. These ideas position you to project three years into the future and imagine what needs to be true about your life in order to be satisfied with your progress. To learn more, check out his book, *The Dan Sullivan Question: Ask It and Transform Anyone's Future.*

- What needs to occur for you to be satisfied with your financial progress?

4. **Elaborate a One-Year Plan.** With the vision clearly set and milestones defined, build a plan of action to move you in the right direction over a period of twelve months.

   - What processes and disciplines do you need to implement in pursuit of your milestones and vision?
   - What simple first steps can you take to gain momentum?
   - Do any obstacles need to be removed to lay the groundwork for your vision?
   - How will you track your progress?
   - Who will help to keep you accountable in pursuit of your plan?

Planning doesn't have to be intimidating. By starting with your vision and outlining the steps to achieve it, you can build a bridge from today to the future you envision. At each step, use the questions above to inform your decisions and gain clarity and direction. Equipped with a framework of goals, milestones, and action steps, you can make your legacy a reality.

Make Planning a Way of Life

Now that you have a planning framework (vision, milestones, one-year plan) in place, you are ready to surround yourself with a team and create processes to make planning a way of life.

Engage Your Team

In Chapter 6 we examined the importance of assembling a multidisciplinary team (legal, tax & accounting, insurance, banking, financial) to provide you with wise counsel. The planning framework gives structure and direction to what you and the team aim to accomplish. The team's collective and strategic wisdom coupled with your willingness to act produces a powerful synergy.

Set a Cadence of Planning

Throughout the book we've continually reinforced the importance of planning. As I stated in Chapter 6, your plan should be a living document. Your life is dynamic. This world is dynamic. Your planning needs to be dynamic as well.

- **Progress check and accountability** (quarterly or semi-annually). Two to four times a year you should connect with your financial advisor to ensure you are on track to achieve the targets in your one-year plan. Members of the team can be incorporated into these discussions to provide relevant expertise.
- **Plan refresh and realignment** (annually). Once a year you'll want to review the one-year plan and develop the next year's plan. This is also a good time to review the milestones and vision and adapt it based upon changes in your life and priorities.

These periodic accountability meetings to evaluate progress, as well as the annual strategy sessions to adjust the plan and milestones, allow you to operate in a continual planning process that adapts your roadmap throughout your life.

Legacy by the Decades

With each passing decade, you are different and your life is different, therefore your planning should be different. Bobb Biehl says in *Decade by Decade*, "All planning, personal and organizational, begins with [the] phrase: 'at this phase of life.'"[4] In Chapter 4 we explored how legacy building and life planning change over time, focusing on survival and success in your twenties and thirties, hitting your stride in your fifties, simplifying in your eighties, and passing on your story in your nineties. For those who want to see financial benchmarks and quantitative measures alongside the more qualitative planning concepts, our website documents net worth and savings targets for each decade.[5]

The path is clear: Begin with gratitude, establish a framework for planning, and utilize a team of advisors to keep you accountable to planning throughout your life.

Legacy Planning Checklist

Whether you tackle financial planning in a DIY fashion or partner with an advisory team, a checklist helps to clarify the essential tasks.

___ Go B.I.G.

___ Find your passion and identity separate from work.

___ Set an aspirational vision (twenty or more years out).

___ Define a key milestone half-way toward the vision.

___ Define an incremental milestone part way to the key.

___ Elaborate a one-year plan with clear objectives.

___ Assemble a team of professionals to guide you.

___ Implement a cadence of accountability and planning.

___ Adapt the focus of your planning process by decade.

If you find this checklist helpful and you'd like more templates, checklists, videos, and guides, you can request your **Work Optional Lifestyle Starter Kit** by sending an email to kyle@legendsdontretire.com.

Get in Motion

"An object in motion tends to remain in motion along a straight line unless acted upon by an outside force." Sir Isaac Newton discovered that once something starts moving, it tends to keep moving. This is true for physics, but it's also true for human behavior.

As you read the previous checklist, it's easy to feel overwhelmed and to delay action. According to productivity expert David Allen, the key to breaking through procrastination is to identify the "next action," a concrete activity that moves the project or task closer to completion. Allen contends a lack of clarity leads to analysis paralysis. "Things rarely get stuck because of lack of time. They get stuck because the doing of them has not been defined."[6]

To get in motion, identify that initial concrete step to move your plan forward. That could be setting an appointment with your financial advisory team. Maybe your next action involves talking with your spouse about your vision and goals. Perhaps you just need to block time in your schedule for soul searching and journaling to discover the legacy you want to live.

Gratitude in Motion

Be grateful and take action. With those two elements, you're well on your way to a meaningful life.

As Luke Skywalker learned, you can't wait until you have everything figured out. Once you have a strategic framework in place, you're going to have to trust your heart (The Force), lean on your team (The Rebels) and embark upon the adventure of a lifetime (take on The Empire). It's time to get moving. Your legacy awaits.

Legendary Questions

1. Go BIG. What are you most grateful for personally or professionally over the past 90 days?

2. Utilizing the Legacy Planning Checklist, what legacy-building activities do you intend to prioritize over the next 90 days?

3. What concrete action can you take today or this week to get in motion and move your legacy forward?

Appendix

Frequently Asked Questions

My whole life I've been told to focus on saving for retirement. Are you saying I must work forever?

Saving for your future is a terrific idea. I'm a big fan. The effect of compound interest is too powerful to forego. As for work, I don't want anyone to work a day longer than they choose. It is the freedom to choose that I am most passionate about cultivating.

I aim to challenge the classic notion of working relentlessly for four decades, striving toward some arbitrary accumulation of assets without fully pursuing your passions and building your legacy. That's why I advocate a Work Optional Lifestyle to strike a balance between spending needs, faucets of income, and buckets of assets, which are all structured to give you freedom of choice. If you want to work, more power to you. If work no longer fulfills you, you're free to follow your heart rather than a paycheck.

I'm already in or near retirement. Is it too late for me to plan?

I get this question a lot. It's never too late to engage in financial planning. When you do so later in the life, your options are more limited, but the value of planning does not diminish.

Planning, even when done closer to your retirement, allows you to evaluate a wide range of considerations, including:

1. Social Security & Income Planning

- Should you claim Social Security early, at your Full Retirement Age (FRA) or delay in order to maximize the monthly benefit amount?
- If you are married, should both spouses utilize the same Social Security claiming strategy, or is it more beneficial for one to claim early or at FRA while the other spouse delays their benefit claim?
- How should you layer other income streams over time in order to maximize return and meet spending needs?
- How should your income planning adjust to account for rising inflation over the years?

2. Healthcare Planning

- When do you need to enroll in Medicare?
- Should you enroll in Part A and Part B of Medicare or only one?
- When does it make sense to enroll in Part D for prescription drug coverage?
- If you have an HSA, should it be used to cover all healthcare costs or only certain ones?
- What is the most effective way to pay for long-term care?

3. Estate Planning

- Does your family need a trust, or is a will sufficient?
- If you do need a trust, what's the right kind for your needs?
- How can you ensure your family doesn't have to deal with probate after you pass?
- What is the most tax efficient way to transfer your assets to heirs?
- Should you hand off portions of your estate over time or disperse all of it at death?
- How can you ensure your charitable giving goals are met?

There are a lot of planning considerations. Addressing them later in life is far superior to never addressing them at all. The best time to plant a tree was twenty years ago. The second-best time is today.

With low-cost investing options so readily available, why shouldn't I handle this all on my own?

If financial success could be achieved by simply generating a reasonable return on an investment portfolio, then handling your finances solo might make sense. However, the benefit of sound advice extends beyond investment counseling.

A financial advisor will coach you on key disciplines, such as cashflow optimization and tax diversification. More importantly, your advisor serves as a behavioral coach to encourage you to make wise decisions even when your emotions tell you otherwise. It's like having a personal trainer, but for your finances.

Finally, your advisor acts as quarterback for your team. Instead of the various specialists on your team pulling you in multiple directions, your financial advisor melds the other team members' advice into a cohesive gameplan, ensuring a clear and consistent direction for your financial future.

I don't trust the stock market. Are there ways to achieve a Work Optional Lifestyle that don't involve stocks and bonds?

Absolutely! If your advisor talks with you about only market-based investment mechanisms, then you may want to consider a different advisor. Financial planning is broader than investment counseling alone, and more than one path exists for generating the necessary income for your spending targets.

If the stock market doesn't appeal to you, consider the following options for a robust income plan:

- Building a business
- Dividend income (stock-based, but with predictable income)
- Interest from a bond ladder (the bond market operates differently than the stock market)
- Investment real estate (short-term rentals, long-term rentals, and commercial real estate)

- Private lending (gap financing; small business lending; peer-to-peer lending through companies such as Lending Club, Prosper, or Upstart)
- Various insurance vehicles

A Work Optional Lifestyle doesn't have to depend on the whims of the stock market. There are multiple avenues available.

Finding the right financial advisory team to trust is scary. What questions should I ask?

It's vital to thoroughly vet any prospective financial advisory team. Some important questions you should ask include:

- Do you serve as a fiduciary* for your clients?
- How do you get paid? Does that compensation ever hinge on certain products being purchased?
- What is the cost of advice versus the all-in† cost of implementing that advice?
- What is your financial planning process?
- What is your investment implementation process?
- Do you specialize in a particular client niche?

---

*A fiduciary is someone who acts on behalf of another, often in matters of law or finance. Fiduciaries are duty-bound to place the interests of another above their own. They have a Duty of Care, Duty of Loyalty, and Duty to Act in Good Faith.

†Anytime you are discussing investment costs associated with implementing advice, make sure you understand the "all-in" cost. This should include transaction costs as well as internal expense ratios. The total cost may be much higher than you realize.

- How do you keep your clients on track to achieve their goals?
- What investment benchmarks do you use when implementing advice for a client?
- What expectations do you have of clients you serve?

The most important thing is to find a team you trust to act in your best interest. Look for a team of professionals who value open communication and who are willing to partner with you and your family in stewarding not only your finances but also your legacy.

About Bluegrass Legacy Group

When my grandfather returned from serving in WWII, he used the G.I. Bill to finance a farm in rural Kentucky ("The Bluegrass State"). I have so many fond memories of time on the farm with my grandfather. "Pappaw," as we called him, came from a different era. He embraced traditional values of hard work, discipline, and frugality.

He built his wealth the old-fashioned way: one cow and one stack of tobacco at a time. Diversification meant spreading his money between every bank and brokerage across three counties. But when he was ready to sell the farm and retire, he consolidated his assets with a single financial advisor whom he trusted. Everyone should have a trusted advisor.

Pappaw passed down a legacy of investing, but he invested in more than just stocks and bonds. He invested in people, his community, and his faith. He passed this legacy of old-school values to my father and eventually to me. I started this firm to continue that tradition.

At Bluegrass Legacy Group, we partner with you to define the legacy you want to leave, organize your assets to accomplish this vision, and hold you accountable to turn your goals into reality.

When considering a wealth management team, it is important to realize the grass isn't always greener. In fact, it can be better: it can be **blue**.

BLUEGRASS
LEGACY GROUP
turning lives into legacies

www.bluegrasslegacygroup.com

About Kyle

Most financial advisors are burdened with hair and the personality of a toaster. They drown you in charts, graphs, and industry jargon. Not Kyle. Instead, he will explain financial concepts in practical ways, tell a few terrible dad jokes, share the bald truth regarding your financial outlook, and help you craft a lasting legacy like the one his grandfather and father passed to him.

From a young age, Kyle has been passionate about finance, business, and problem solving. After studying economics at the University of Arlington, he built a fifteen-year career consulting with Fortune 500 companies in the finance, insurance, and defense sectors. In 2014, he began serving individual investors as an advisor at Edward Jones. When the economy and the industry experienced significant stress in 2020, Kyle formed Bluegrass Legacy Group to better serve his clients and provide a more responsive, higher level of care.

Kyle and his team specialize in serving business owners, entrepreneurs, families, and nonprofits. He loves the uniqueness of individuals and organizations, and he passionately pursues their vision for legacy.

A proud native Texan, father of six, and grandfather of one, Kyle is an avid board and card game player. His tenacity is demonstrated through soccer and testing his limits with endurance challenges including 75 Hard, Tough Mudder, and the Spartan Trifecta. When not serving his clients, Kyle enjoys spending time with his children and traveling with the love of his life, Tammy.

Marriage ministry is one of many passions he and his wife Tammy share. Together they lead Equip Your Marriage, a faith-based ministry dedicated to empowering and equipping couples to unlock the incredible potential within a vibrant partnership. Through books, workshops, and hands-on mentoring, they minister to couples from their home base in Texas. You can learn more at http://www.equipyourmarriage.com.

Whether coaching clients or mentoring couples, Kyle is committed to stewarding the gifts he has been given and helping others do the same.

Notes

Introduction

1. *Spider-Man*, directed by Sam Raimi (Columbia Pictures Corporation & Marvel Enterprises, 2002).

Chapter One

1. "Research Note #3: Details of Ida May Fuller's Payroll Tax Contributions," Social Security Administration, accessed June 20, 2022, https://www.ssa.gov/history/idapayroll.html.

2. "Life Expectancy (from Birth) in the United States, from 1860 to 2020," Statista, accessed June 20, 2022. https://www.statista.com/statistics/1040079/life-expectancy-united-states-all-time/.

3. "Ratio of Covered Workers to Beneficiaries," Social Security Administration, accessed June 20, 2022, https://www.ssa.gov/history/ratios.html.

4. Ibid. *See also*: Smart Asset's online Inflation Calculator, https://smartasset.com/investing/inflation-calculator.

5. Renee Stepler, "World's Centenarian Population Projected to Grow Eightfold by 2050," Pew Research Center, April 21, 2016, https://www.pewresearch.org/fact-tank/2016/04/21/worlds-centenarian-population-projected-to-grow-eightfold-by-2050/.

6. Mary-Lou Weisman, "The History of Retirement, From Early Man to AARP," *New York Times*, March 21, 1999.

7. Dan Sullivan, *My Plan for Living to 156* (Toronto: The Strategic Coach, 2018), 27.

Chapter Two

1. *Merriam-Webster*, s.v. "legacy (*n.*)," accessed July 12, 2022, https://www.merriam-webster.com/dictionary/legacy.

2. Peter Strople (@pstrople), "Legacy is not leaving something for people. It's leaving something in people," Twitter, August 23, 2018, 9:48 a.m., https://twitter.com/ pstrople/status/1032640745142935552 ?lang=en.

3. Vicki Robin & Joe Dominguez, *Your Money or Your Life: 9 Steps to Transforming Your Relationship with Money and Achieving Financial Independence*, (London: Penguin, 2018).

4. "FIRE Explained," Playing with Fire, accessed June 22, 2022, https://www.playingwithfire.co/whatisfire.

Chapter Three

1. Christian Soschner, "Did Einstein Ever Say Compound Interest is the 8th Wonder of the World?" *Medium*, August 19, 2021, https://medium.datadriveninvestor.com/did-einstein-ever-say-compound-interest-is-the-8th-wonder-of-the-world-75ca2f200dd7.

2. Sheiresa Ngo, "New Job? Don't Forget Your Finances," *Wall St. Watchdog*, September 6, 2018, https://www.wallstwatchdog.com/money-career/new-job-dont-forget-your-finances/.

3. Margarette Burnette, "Compound Interest Calculator," *Nerd Wallet*, August 1, 2022,

https://www.nerdwallet.com/banking/calculator/compound-interest-calculator.

4. Rob Shikina, "Oldest female marathoner dies at 100," *Star Advertiser*, November 11, 2019, https://www.staradvertiser.com/2019/11/11/hawaii-news/oldest-female-marathoner-dies-at-100/.

5. "Julia Child," PBS.org, accessed August 6th, 2022, https://www.pbs.org/food/chefs/julia-child/.

6. "The birthplace of instant noodles," Cup Noodles Museum, accessed August 6th, 2022, https://www.cupnoodles-museum.jp/en/osaka_ikeda/about/.

7. "Peter Mark Roget," Britannica.com, accessed August 6th, 2022, https://www.britannica.com/biography/Peter-Mark-Roget.

8. "Grandma Moses Biography," A&E Television Networks, April 2, 2014, accessed August 6th, 2022, https://www.biography.com/artist/grandma-moses.

9. "Biography of Nelson Mandela," Nelson Mandela Foundation, accessed August 6th, 2022, https://www.nelsonmandela.org/content/page/biography.

10. "Ray Croc: Burger Baron," *Entrepreneur*, October 9, 2008, accessed August 6th, 2022, https://www.entrepreneur.com/article/197544.

11. Shigeyoshi Kimura, "100-Year-Old Conquers Mount Fuji," *AP News*, August 2, 1987, https://apnews.com/article/7bca40602fb4c2b2b9468f2815d530c7

12. Attributed to John Stuart Mill in *The Phrenological Journal and Science of Health*, Vol. LXXXV (September 1887), 170,

https://quotepark.com/quotes/1002100-john-stuart-mill-i-have-learned-to-seek-my-happiness-by-limiting-my/

13. Walter Mischel and Ebbe B. Ebbesen, "Attention in Delay of Gratification," *Journal of Personality and Social Psychology* 16 no. 2 (1970): 329–337, https://doi.org/10.1037/h0029815.

14. Mischel, W; Shoda, Y; Rodriguez, M. (26 May 1989). "Delay of gratification in children". Science. 244 (4907): 933–938, https://doi.org/:10.1126/science.2658056.

15. Ozlem N Ayduk, et al., "Regulating the Interpersonal Self: Strategic Self-Regulation for Coping with Rejection Sensitivity," *Journal of Personality and Social Psychology*. 79 no. 5 (December 2000): 776–92, https://doi.org/10.1037//0022-3514.79.5.776.

16. Tanya R. Schlam, et al., "Preschoolers' Delay of Gratification Predicts Their Body Mass 30 Years Later," *Journal of Pediatrics* 162 no. 1 (January 2013): 1–218, https://doi.org/10.1016/j.jpeds.2012.06.049.

17. Elizabeth Warren and Amelia Warren Tyagi, *All Your Worth: The Ultimate Lifetime Money Plan* (New York: Free Press, 2005).

18. Dave Ramsey, *The Total Money Makeover: A Proven Plan for Financial Fitness*, 2nd ed. (Nashville: Thomas Nelson, 2007).

19. William Feather, *The Business of Life* (New York: Simon and Schuster, 1949), 75.

Chapter Four

1. Bobb Biehl, Decade by Decade: Life Is Surprisingly Predictable (Scottsdale: Aylen Publishing, 2020).

2. Biehl, *Decade*, 51.

3. Biehl, *Decade*, 49.

4. James Clear, *Atomic Habits: Tiny Changes, Remarkable Results : An Easy & Proven Way to Build Good Habits & Break Bad Ones* (New York: Penguin Random House, 2018), 16.

Chapter Five

1. Stephen Tomkins, *David Livingstone: The Unexplored Story.* (Oxford, England: Lion Books, 2013).

2. "Harry Truman," *Best Quotations,* accessed August 8, 2022, https://best-quotations.com/authquotes.php?auth=130.

3. "4 Questions To Help You Define Your Legacy," PeopleResults, August 5, 2013, https://www.people-results.com/4-questions-define-legacy/.

4 Dawn Franks, "How Life Stories Become the Legacy You Leave," LinkedIn, October 16, 2020, https://www.linkedin.com/pulse/how-life-stories-become-legacy-you-leave-dawn-franks/.

5. "How to Make a Positive Impact: Giving Back to Make a Positive Impact and Improve Your Community," Tony Robbins (website), accessed on June 30, 2022, https://www.tonyrobbins.com/leadership-impact/10-easy-ways-to-make-a-big-impact/.

6. John R. Stott, *The Living Church: Convictions of a Lifelong Pastor* (Downers Grove: InterVarsity Press, 2007).

7. Jeanie A. B. Greenough, *A Year of Beautiful Thoughts (1902)* (Whitefish, MT: Kessinger Publishing, 2010), 172.

Chapter Six

1. United Press International, "Photographer Carl McCunn, Stranded and Starving in the Alaskan Wilderness, Shot Himself out of Desperation to End the Ordeal, His Diary Showed," December 13, 1982, https://www.upi.com/Archives/1982/12/13/Photographer-Carl-McCunn-stranded-and-starving-in-the-Alaskan/7238408603600/.

2. Associated Press, "Left in Man Penned Dying Record," *New York Times*, December 19, 1982, https://www.nytimes.com/1982/12/19/us/left-in-wilds-man-penned-dying-record.html.

3. Chris M. Merritt, "Mount Everest Deaths Statistics by Year (1922-2019)," *Outdoor Inquirer*, accessed July 1, 2022, https://outdoorinquirer.com/mount-everest-deaths/.

4. Paul G. Firth, et al., "Mortality on Mount Everest, 1921-2006: Descriptive Study," *British Medical Journal*, 337 (2008): a2654, https://doi.org/10.1136/bmj.a2654.

5. Hillary Brueck, "A Mount Everest Record-Holder Says Summit 'Traffic Jams' Aren't the Problem—It's the Trek Down That Kills People," *Business Insider*, June 1, 2019, https://www.businessinsider.com/mount-everest-record-holder-trek-down-deaths-2019-5.

6. "HR 4591 VA Electronic Health Record Transparency Act of 2021," June 23, 2022, Internal Revenue Code. Public Law 117-154, https://www.congress.gov/bill/117th-congress/house-bill/4591.

7. Harry Markowitz, "Portfolio Selection," *Journal of Finance*, vol 7, no. 1 (1952).

8. The Royal Swedish Academy of Sciences, "This Year's Laureates Are Pioneers in the Theory of Financial Economics and Corporate Finance," news release, October 16, 1990, https://www.nobelprize.org/prizes/economic-sciences/1990/press-release/.

9. Yogi Berra and David Kaplan, *When You Come to a Fork in the Road, Take It!: Inspiration and Wisdom from One of Baseball's Greatest Heroes* (New York: Hachette Books, 2002), 53.

10. Stephen R. Covey, *The 7 Habits of Highly Effective People: Restoring the Character Ethic* (New York: Free Press 2004).

11. Zig Ziglar (@TheZigZiglar), "It's not where you start that matters. It's where you finish that counts," Twitter, August 18, 2013, 11:35 p.m., https://twitter.com/TheZigZiglar/status/369316709703757824.

12. Fidelity Viewpoints, "How to plan for rising health care costs," Fidelity, May 25, 2022, https://www.fidelity.com/viewpoints/personal-finance/plan-for-rising-health-care-costs.

13. Administration for Community Living, "How much care will you need?" LongTermCare.gov, accessed July 5, 2022, https://acl.gov/ltc/basic-needs/how-much-care-will-you-need.

Chapter Seven

1. *Star Wars: Episode V—The Empire Strikes Back* directed by Irvin Kershner (United States: Lucasfilm, 1980).

2. Melody Beattie, *The Language of Letting Go (Hazelden Meditation Series)* (United States: Hazelden Publishing, 1990), 163.

3. Bobb Biehl, *Decade by Decade: Life Is Surprisingly Predictable* (Scottsdale: Aylen Publishing, 2020), 50–51.

4. Biehl, *Decade,* 16.

5. "Legacy by the Decades," Bluegrass Legacy Group, accessed August 8, 2022, https://bluegrasslegacygroup.com/legacy-by-the-decades/.

6. David Allen, *Getting Things Done*, (London: Piatkus Books, 2002).

WHAT'S NEXT?

DO YOU HAVE A GROUP/EVENT THAT YOU'D LIKE TO HAVE KYLE KYLE SPEAK AT?

DO YOU HAVE A PODCAST THAT YOU'D LIKE KYLE TO BE A PART OF?

WOULD YOU LIKE TO LEARN MORE ABOUT BLUEGRASS LEGACY GROUP?

VISIT WWW.LEGENDSDONTRETIRE.COM

BE SURE TO GET YOUR WORK OPTIONAL STARTER KIT

WHAT'S INCLUDED?

- LEGACY VISION WORKSHEET TO CLARIFY YOUR GOALS
- PLANNING FRAMEWORK TO DEFINE YOUR MILESTONES
- BUDGETING TEMPLATES TO OPTIMIZE YOUR CASHFLOW
- ACCOUNTABILITY CHECKLISTS TO KEEP YOU ON TRACK

TO RECEIVE YOUR STARTER KIT, PLEASE EMAIL KYLE@LEGENDSDONTRETIRE.COM

Copyright © 2022 by Robert Kyle Gabhart